NATIONAL GEOGRAPHIC LEARNING | CENGAGE Learning

READING
EXPLORER

2

PAUL MACINTYRE • DAVID BOHLKE

Second Edition

NATIONAL GEOGRAPHIC LEARNING | CENGAGE Learning

Australia • Brazil • Japan • Korea • Mexico • Singapore • Spain • United Kingdom • United States

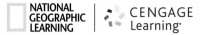

Reading Explorer 2
Second Edition

Paul MacIntyre and David Bohlke

Publisher: Andrew Robinson

Executive Editor: Sean Bermingham

Senior Development Editor: Derek Mackrell

Development Editor: Claire Tan

Director of Global Marketing: Ian Martin

Product Marketing Manager: Lindsey Miller

Senior Content Project Manager: Tan Jin Hock

Manufacturing Planner: Mary Beth Hennebury

Compositor: SPi Global

Cover/Text Design: Creative Director: Christopher Roy, Art Director: Scott Baker, Designer: Alex Dull

Cover Photo: Frans Lanting/ National Geographic Creative

For permission to use material from this text or product, submit all requests online at **cengage.com/permissions**
Further permissions questions can be emailed to **permissionrequest@cengage.com**

Student Book with Online Workbook:
ISBN-13: 978-1-305-25447-3

Student Book:
ISBN-13: 978-1-285-84690-3

National Geographic Learning
20 Channel Center Street
Boston, MA 02210
USA

Cengage Learning is a leading provider of customized learning solutions with office locations around the globe, including Singapore, the United Kingdom, Australia, Mexico, Brazil, and Japan. Locate your local office at: **international.cengage.com/region**

Cengage Learning products are represented in Canada by Nelson Education, Ltd.

Visit National Geographic Learning online at **NGL.Cengage.com**

Visit our corporate website at **www.cengage.com**

Printed in the United States

8 9 10 11 12   22 21 20 19 18

Contents

Scope and Sequence

Reading Skill	Vocabulary Building	Video
A: Skimming for the Main Idea of Paragraphs **B:** Identifying the Purpose of Paragraphs	**A:** Word Partnership: *cut down on* **B:** Word Link: *-ance*	Olive Oil
A: Understanding Pronoun Reference **B:** Scanning for Details	**A:** Thesaurus: *leap* **B:** Thesaurus: *talent*	Man's Best Friend
A: Creating a Timeline of Events **B:** Distinguishing Facts from Theories	**A:** Word Link: *teen* **B:** Word Partnership: *debate*	Inca Mummy
A: Dealing with Unfamiliar Vocabulary **B:** Differentiating Between Main Ideas and Supporting Details	**A:** Word Link: *re-* **B:** Word Link: *en-*	Aboriginal Rock Art
A: Understanding the Functions of Prepositional Phrases **B:** Breaking Down Long Sentences	**A:** Word Partnership: *trend* **B:** Thesaurus: *awful*	Sewer Diver
A: Understanding Cause and Effect Relationships **B:** Recognizing Contrastive Relationships	**A:** Word Partnership: *negative* **B:** Word Link: *in-*	Swimming with Sharks
A: Determining Similarities and Differences **B:** Understanding Synonyms	**A:** Word Partnership: *handle* **B:** Word Partnership: *obtain*	Madagascar Perfume
A: Understanding Time Clauses/Time Relationships **B:** Recognizing Participle Clauses	**A:** Word Partnership: *undertake* **B:** Thesaurus: *remote*	The Legend of Marco Polo
A: Evaluating Claims **B:** Understanding Inference	**A:** Word Partnership: *reward* **B:** Thesaurus: *severe*	The Global Village
A: Identifying Types of Supporting Details **B:** Identifying an Author's Tone or Point of View	**A:** Word Partnership: *host* **B:** Usage: *I'm starving!*	Greenland's Melting Glaciers
A: Understanding Prefixes and Suffixes **B:** Summarizing a Text	**A:** Word Link: *co-* **B:** Word Partnership: *reaction*	Kenya Butterflies
A: Recognizing Similes **B:** Synthesizing Information from Multiple Sources	**A:** Word Partnership: *thrill* **B:** Word Partnership: *necessity*	Sky Shooter

Welcome to Reading Explorer!

In this book, you'll travel the globe, explore different cultures, and discover new ways of looking at the world. You'll also become a better reader!

What's new in the Second Edition?

New and updated topics

Explore secret cities, kung fu temples, and the amazing human brain.

New Reading Skills section

Learn how to read strategically—and think critically as you read.

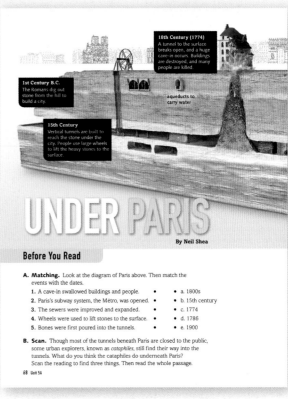

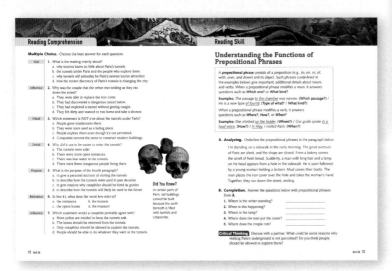

Expanded Viewing section

Apply your language skills when you watch a specially adapted National Geographic video.

Now you're ready

to explore your world!

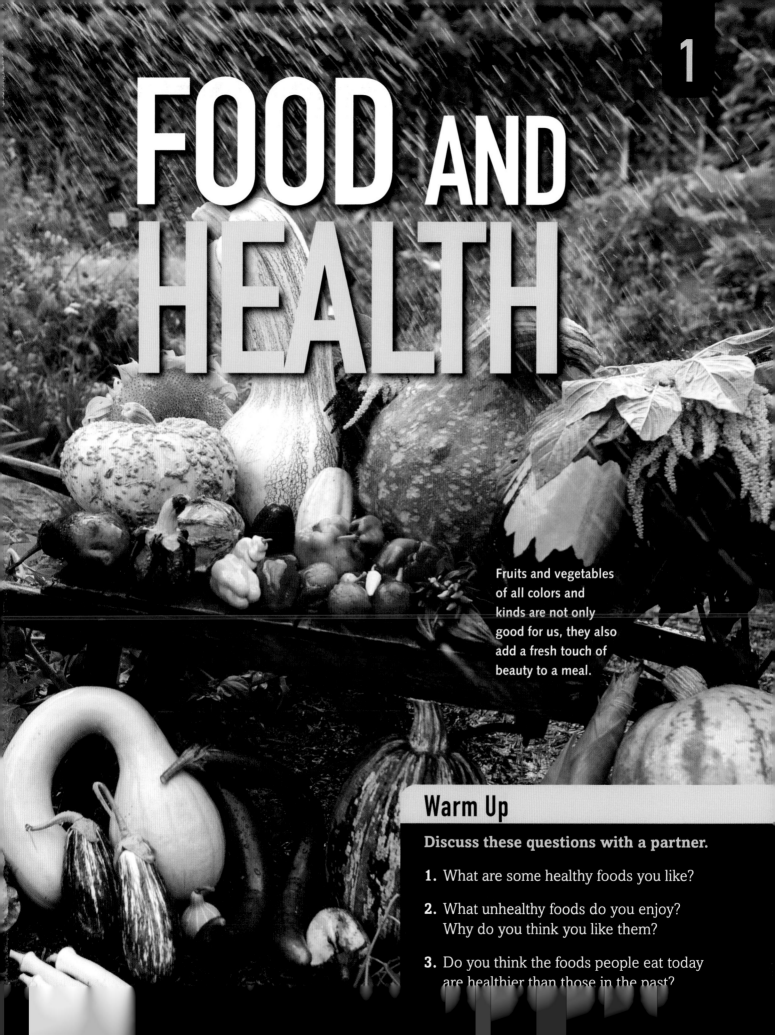

FOOD AND HEALTH

Fruits and vegetables of all colors and kinds are not only good for us, they also add a fresh touch of beauty to a meal.

Warm Up

Discuss these questions with a partner.

1. What are some healthy foods you like?

2. What unhealthy foods do you enjoy? Why do you think you like them?

3. Do you think the foods people eat today are healthier than those in the past?

SWEET LOVE

Before You Read

Sugary treats come in all kinds.

A. Matching. How much sugar do you think is in these foods? Match the items below to the correct amount of sugar. Then check your answers at the bottom of page 10.

1. yogurt • • a. 3 grams
2. 3 chocolate cookies • • b. 10 grams
3. wheat squares cereal • • c. 13 grams
4. 1 cupcake with frosting • • d. 25 grams
5. 2 slices of wheat bread • • e. 27 grams

B. Scan. Why do you think people love sugar so much? Discuss with a partner. Then scan the first paragraph on page 9 to check your ideas.

Why do we love sugar so much?

Many scientists believe our love of sugar may actually be an **addiction**. When we eat or drink sugary foods, the sugar enters our blood and affects parts of our brain that make us feel good. Then the good feeling goes away, leaving us wanting more. All tasty foods do this, but sugar has a particularly strong effect. In this way, it is in fact an addictive **drug**, one that doctors **recommend** we all **cut down on**.

"It seems like every time I study an illness and trace a path to the first cause, I find my way back to sugar," says scientist Richard Johnson. One-third of adults worldwide have high blood pressure,[1] and up to 347 million have diabetes.[2] Why? "Sugar, we believe, is one of the culprits, if not the major culprit," says Johnson.

Our bodies are designed to survive on very little sugar. Early humans often had very little food, so our bodies learned to be very **efficient** in **storing** sugar as fat. In this way, we had energy stored for when there was no food. But today, most people have more than enough. So the very thing that once saved us may now be killing us.

So what is the solution? It's **obvious** that we need to eat less sugar. The trouble is, in today's world, it's extremely difficult to avoid. From breakfast cereals to after-dinner desserts, our foods are increasingly filled with it. Some manufacturers even use sugar to replace taste in foods that are **advertised** as low in fat.

But there are those who are fighting back against sugar. Many schools are replacing sugary desserts with healthier options like fruit. Other schools are growing their own food in gardens, or building **facilities** like walking tracks so students and others in the community can exercise. The **battle** has not yet been lost.

---

1 A person with **high blood pressure** has blood flowing through his or her body at higher than normal pressure, which can lead to a number of diseases.

2 **Diabetes** is a medical condition in which someone has too much sugar in his or her blood.

Many believe the lollipop was first invented in the Middle Ages. The largest lollipop created in modern times weighed 3,176 kilograms.

Reading Comprehension

Multiple Choice. Choose the best answer for each question.

Gist
1. What is this passage mainly about?
   a. our addiction to sugar
   b. illnesses caused by sugar
   c. good sugar vs. bad sugar
   d. ways to avoid sugar

Vocabulary
2. In line 17, the word *culprit* is closest in meaning to _____.
   a. disease   b. unknown thing
   c. sweet food   d. cause of the problem

Reference
3. What does the phrase *the very thing* in line 22 refer to?
   a. the amount of sugar in our food
   b. having enough food to survive
   c. our ability to store sugar as fat
   d. early humans' lack of food

Main Idea
4. What would be a good title for the fourth paragraph?
   a. Too Much Sugar
   b. How to Avoid Sugar
   c. A Solution: Low in Fat
   d. No Easy Answers

Detail
5. According to the passage, why is it so hard to avoid sugar?
   a. We like candy too much.
   b. It gives us needed energy.
   c. It's in so many foods and drinks.
   d. We get used to eating it at school.

Detail
6. Which of the following statements about sugar is NOT true?
   a. Sugar makes us feel good.
   b. Our bodies store sugar as fat.
   c. We need very little sugar to survive.
   d. Only adults need to stop eating sugar.

Cohesion
7. The following sentence would best be placed at the end of which paragraph? *This may make the food appear as healthier, but large amounts of sugar are often added.*
   a. paragraph 1   b. paragraph 2
   c. paragraph 3   d. paragraph 4

Did You Know?

Doctors recommend we eat no more than 9.5 teaspoons of sugar a day, but studies show the average person eats around 22.7 teaspoons.

Answers to Before You Read A:
1. 27 g, 2. 10 g, 3. 13 g, 4. 25 g, 5. 3 g

Skimming for the Main Idea of Paragraphs

When you read a text, it's important to be able to recognize the main idea of each paragraph. Look at the headings (if there are any) and skim each paragraph to determine the key idea the author is making. When you skim, you don't read every word. Instead, read the first sentence and then run your eyes quickly over the rest, focusing on key words.

Make sure you are finding the main idea of the whole paragraph. Other sentences may express an idea, but it may not be the main idea.

∧ While fresh fruits do contain small amounts of sugar, they make a healthy snack.

A. Determining Main Ideas. Look back at the passage on page 9. Choose the main idea of each paragraph.

1. **Paragraph 1**
   a. Sugar is addictive.
   b. All tasty foods contain sugar.

2. **Paragraph 2**
   a. Sugar can cause illnesses.
   b. The number of people with diabetes and high blood pressure is rising.

3. **Paragraph 3**
   a. Sugar gives us energy when we don't eat for a long time.
   b. Our bodies need very little sugar to survive, but we now eat too much of it.

4. **Paragraph 4**
   a. Advertisers are being dishonest.
   b. It is very difficult to avoid sugar these days.

5. **Paragraph 5**
   a. Some schools now grow their own food.
   b. Some are fighting back against sugar.

Critical Thinking Discuss with a partner. Do you think manufacturers have a responsibility to reduce the amount of sugar in the products they sell? Why or why not?

Vocabulary Practice

A. Completion. Complete the information below with the correct form of words in the box. Two words are extra.

addiction	battle	drug	recommend	store

The story of sugar began in New Guinea about 10,000 years ago. People there picked sugarcane and ate it raw. Because it made people feel good, they saw it as a(n) **1.** _____ that could cure illnesses. Doctors in India **2.** _____ that people eat it to stop headaches. But soon people began to eat it for fun. Demand for sugar rose, as more people became **3.** _____ to the sweet taste. By 1900, it was recorded that the average British person ate 45 kilograms (100 pounds) of sugar each year.

B. Words in Context. Complete each sentence with the correct answer.

1. When a company **advertises** something, they want you to _____ it.
   a. return   b. buy

2. Someone who is **efficient** at a task does the task without _____.
   a. spending a lot of money   b. wasting time or energy

3. Two groups that have a **battle** are likely to be _____ each other.
   a. friendly with   b. angry at

4. The **facilities** of a school include the _____.
   a. classrooms   b. teachers

5. If something is **obvious**, it is easy to _____.
   a. find a mistake with it   b. see or understand

6. When you **store** something, you _____.
   a. keep it   b. throw it away

7. When you **cut down on** sugar, you eat _____ of it.
   a. less   b. more

> ⌄ A young boy eats a piece of raw sugarcane.

> **Word Partnership**
> Use **cut down on** with: (*n.*) cut down on **sugar**, **fat**, **salt**, **meat**, **drinking**, **smoking**, **living expenses**.

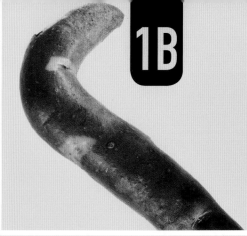

FOOD FOR THE FUTURE

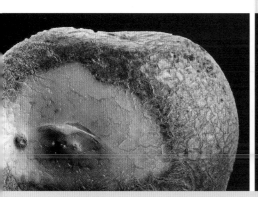

Think all potatoes look and taste alike? Think again. In many countries, people **depend on** a few **species** of "common" potatoes. But potatoes actually come in many different colors and shapes. In Peru and Bolivia, the people **grow** and have **preserved** so many types of potatoes that a whole diet can be built around them.

Before You Read

A. Matching. Look at the pictures and read the text above. Then match the words in **bold** to their definitions.

1. depend on •   • a. to keep safe for future use
2. species   •   • b. to become bigger
3. grow   •   • c. type (usually of plant or animal)
4. preserve   •   • d. to put your trust in something

B. Predict. Look at the picture and captions on pages 14–15. Then read the first paragraph. What do you think the passage is about? Discuss your ideas with a partner. Then read the passage to check your ideas.

Food for the Future

In 1845, a deadly disease struck the farms of Ireland, killing all
the Lumper potato plants. In another place or time, the death of
a single **crop** species might not have been so important. But in
Ireland, in 1845, people depended almost **solely** on the potato
for food. The death of one species caused a terrible famine.[1]
Now, some scientists are worried that such a famine could
happen again—but on a much wider **scale**.

Over the centuries, farmers have discovered thousands of
different species of food crops. Each species has special qualities.
Some can be grown in very hot or cold climates. Others are not
affected by certain diseases. However, you won't find many of
these species in your local supermarket. To feed the seven billion
people on Earth, most farmers today are growing only species
of plants and farming only species of animals that are easy
to produce in large numbers. Meanwhile, thousands of other
species are becoming extinct.[2]

For example, in the Philippines, there were once thousands of
varieties of rice; now fewer than 100 are grown there. In China,
90 percent of the wheat varieties grown just a century ago have
disappeared. Experts believe that over the past century, we have
allowed more than half of the world's food varieties to disappear.

At Heritage Farm's seed
bank, rare and unique
plants are carefully
grown so the seeds
can be preserved and
shared.

1 A **famine** is a situation in
which large numbers of people
have little or no food.

2 If a species becomes **extinct**,
it no longer exists.

Saving the Seeds

One solution to this problem is to collect and preserve the **seeds**
of as many different plant varieties as we can before they disappear.
The idea was first **suggested** by Russian scientist Nikolay Vavilov.
In the 1920s and '30s, he collected around 400,000 seeds from five
continents. More recently, others are continuing the work he began.

In the U.S. state of Iowa, Diane Ott Whealy wanted to preserve
historic plant varieties, like the seeds her great-grandfather brought
to the U.S. from Germany more than a hundred years ago. She and
her husband started a place called Heritage Farm, where people can
store and trade seeds.

More importantly, the people at Heritage Farm don't just store the
seeds; they plant them. By doing this, they are reintroducing foods
into the **marketplace** that haven't been grown for years. These food
species are not just special in terms of appearance or **flavor**. They
also offer farmers food solutions for the future, from the past.

"Heirloom" vegetables, like
these tomatoes, are most often
grown from seeds passed down
and preserved within a unique
community.

Reading Comprehension

Multiple Choice. Choose the best answer for each question.

Gist

1. What is this passage mainly about?
   a. how food species disappear
   b. the need to preserve different food species
   c. what the food we eat will look like someday
   d. ways to increase the number of food species

Cause and Effect

2. What caused many people to die in Ireland in 1845?
   a. The potatoes that people planted didn't grow.
   b. People ate potatoes that were harmful to humans.
   c. A disease killed their potato crop, so they had no food.
   d. A deadly disease spread from the potato crop to humans.

Reference

3. What does the word *others* refer to in line 11?
   a. farmers   b. different climates
   c. distinct qualities   d. species of food crops

Paraphrase

4. Which sentence is closest in meaning to *you won't find many of these species in your local supermarket* (lines 12–13)?
   a. Many of these species are too expensive.
   b. Many of these species are not available to us.
   c. Many of these species look like other species.
   d. Many of these species are only found in big cities.

Detail

5. Which of the following statements is NOT true?
   a. Most farmers grow species that are easy to produce in small numbers.
   b. Thousands of species of plants and animals have become extinct.
   c. Fewer than 100 varieties of rice are grown in the Philippines.
   d. Half of the world's food varieties have disappeared in the past 100 years.

Detail

6. People have been preserving seeds to save crop species and varieties from extinction _____.
   a. for thousands of years   b. for less than 100 years
   c. since 1845   d. for only ten years

Inference

7. Which statement would Diane Ott Whealy probably agree with?
   a. The work started by Nikolay Vavilov was not important.
   b. American seeds are better than German seeds.
   c. It's important to store seeds, but you must also plant them.
   d. Foods grown from older seeds are cheaper, but taste bad.

Did You Know?

From the 307 varieties of corn sold 100 years ago, there are now only 12. Some, including this rare kind of wild corn, exist only in seed banks.

Identifying the Purpose of Paragraphs

Different paragraphs may perform different functions. Identifying their purpose can help you better understand the organization of a text. Some paragraphs may have more than one function. Common purposes include:

- to introduce a topic
- to present a conclusion
- to present an argument
- to summarize the key ideas
- to offer or describe a solution

- to offer another side of an issue
- to describe a situation or problem
- to report data as figures or statistics
- to provide background information
- to provide examples or explanations

A. Purpose. Look back at the passage on pages 14–15. Choose the purpose of each paragraph.

1. Paragraph 1
   a. to provide some historical background
   b. to summarize the key ideas

2. Paragraph 2
   a. to offer another side of the issue
   b. to describe a situation or problem

3. Paragraph 3
   a. to summarize some key ideas
   b. to report data as supporting evidence

4. Paragraph 4
   a. to offer another side of an issue
   b. to offer or describe a solution

5. Paragraph 5
   a. to present an argument
   b. to provide an additional example

6. Paragraph 6
   a. to report data as figures or statistics
   b. to present a concluding idea

⌃ Farmers today don't only preserve plants. They also protect farm animals, like this rare variety of chicken.

Critical Thinking Discuss with a partner. Do you think saving the world's varieties of foods is as important as saving animal species from extinction? Why or why not?

Vocabulary Practice

A. Completion. Circle the correct words to complete the information below.

Today, there are about 1,400 seed banks around the world. These keep seed **1. (varieties / flavors)** from all **2. (marketplaces / continents)** safe in the event of a large **3. (-scale / -historic)** global crisis, such as a famine. One of the largest seed banks lies inside a mountain on Norway's island of Spitsbergen, just 1,300 kilometers from the North Pole. This is a backup for all the world's other seed banks.

In 1996, director Cary Fowler commented that the seed bank's opening "marks a(n) **4. (solely / historic)** turning point in safeguarding the world's **5. (crop / flavor)** diversity." Billions of seeds are now kept there. They are stored in a permanently chilled, earthquake-free zone 120 meters above sea level. This should allow the seeds to remain high and dry, even if the polar ice caps melt.

△ Carved into the Arctic ice, the Svalbard Global Seed Vault holds "spare" copies of seeds held in other seed banks worldwide.

B. Definitions. Match each word in **red** with its definition.

1. _____ **crop**	a.	only
2. _____ **scale**	b.	how something tastes
3. _____ **seed**	c.	to put forward an idea
4. _____ **solely**	d.	important to the past
5. _____ **flavor**	e.	a range of different types
6. _____ **variety**	f.	a place of buying and selling
7. _____ **suggest**	g.	the size or extent of something
8. _____ **historic**	h.	part of a plant from which a new plant grows
9. _____ **continent**	i.	land consisting of countries (e.g., Asia)
10. _____ **marketplace**	j.	a plant grown in large amounts, like wheat

Word Link We can add **-ance** to some verbs to form nouns. Examples include *appearance, performance, attendance, acceptance, assistance, guidance,* and *ignorance.*

VIEWING Olive Oil

Before You Watch

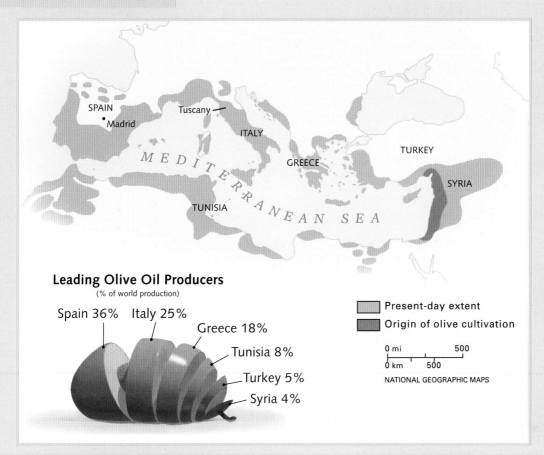

Leading Olive Oil Producers
(% of world production)

Spain 36% Italy 25%
Greece 18%
Tunisia 8%
Turkey 5%
Syria 4%

Present-day extent
Origin of olive cultivation

0 mi   500
0 km   500
NATIONAL GEOGRAPHIC MAPS

A. Warm Up. You are going to watch a video about olive oil. Look at the information above and discuss these questions with a partner.

1. Where were olives first grown for food?
2. Which three countries produce the most olive oil?
3. In what kind of climate do you think olives grow well?

While You Watch

A. True or False. Read the sentences below. As you watch the video, mark these sentences as true (**T**) or false (**F**).

1. To get green olives, you need to collect them when they are young. **T   F**
2. There is a connection between olives and peace. **T   F**
3. Very little of the olive crop in Greece goes to making olive oil. **T   F**
4. You can use olive oil for making light. **T   F**
5. The colors and shapes of the olive trees make Naxos a scary place. **T   F**

After You Watch

A. Completion. Using information from the video, choose the correct word or phrase to complete each sentence.

1. Black and green olives come from (**different trees / the same tree**).

2. It's not easy to identify olive trees without the (**leaves / fruit**).

3. The oldest olive trees are (**hundreds / thousands**) of years old.

4. To produce the best olive oil, (**green / black**) olives are used.

B. Discuss. Discuss these questions with a partner.

1. How often do you have olive oil in your food or use olive oil products?

2. After watching the video, do you think you will start to use more olive oil?

3. What other foods do you know that have health benefits?

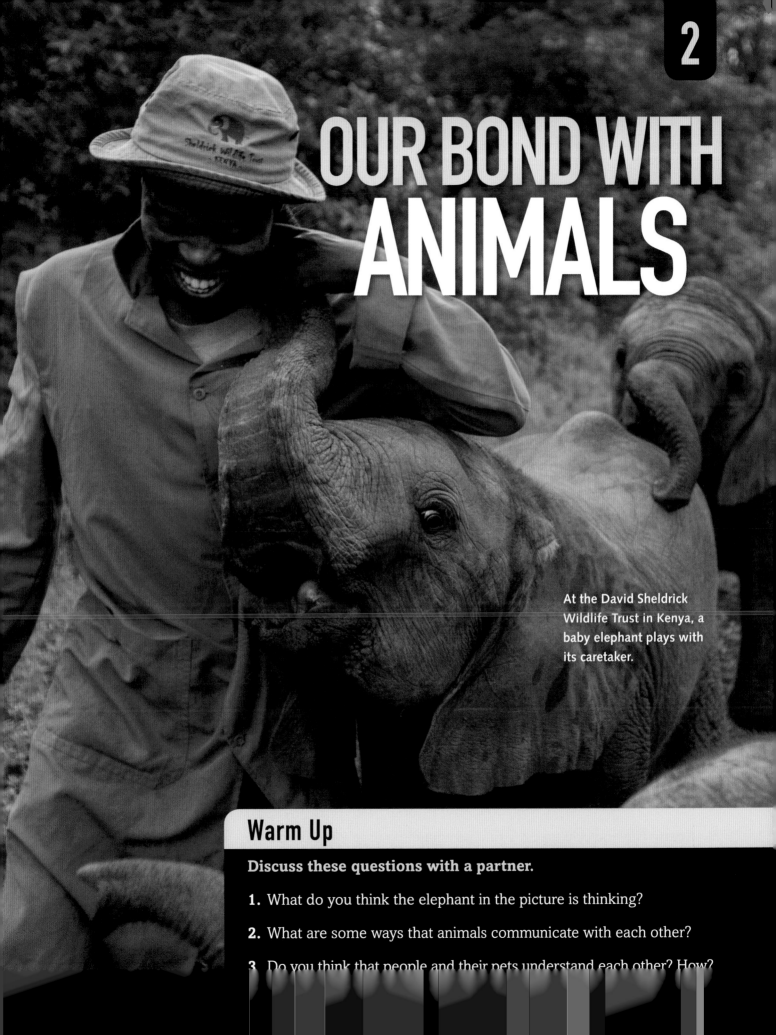

OUR BOND WITH
ANIMALS

At the David Sheldrick
Wildlife Trust in Kenya, a
baby elephant plays with
its caretaker.

Warm Up

Discuss these questions with a partner.

1. What do you think the elephant in the picture is thinking?

2. What are some ways that animals communicate with each other?

3. Do you think that people and their pets understand each other? How?

Before You Read

A. Quiz. The whale in the photo is a humpback. Humpbacks are found in most of the world's oceans. What do you know about them?

1. Humpback whales (**often / rarely**) swim close to land.
2. When a whale breaches, it (**jumps out of / dives deep into**) the water.
3. Humpbacks work together to (**catch fish / attack boats**).
4. Humpback whales talk to each other by (**singing / moving their flippers**).

B. Scan. Now quickly read the first paragraph on page 23 to check your answers. Then read the entire passage.

Humpback whales are powerful swimmers. They use their huge tails to push themselves through the water and sometimes completely out of it. Scientists aren't sure why they do this. Perhaps the whales simply do it for fun.

Song of the Humpback

1 Herman Melville, the writer of the famous whale story *Moby Dick*, once wrote that humpback whales were "the most lighthearted[1] of all the whales." A favorite of whale watchers everywhere, they swim in ocean areas close to land, and are

5 active at the surface. They can often be seen breaching, or **leaping** out of the water, and then coming down with a great splash. Humpbacks are known to be intelligent animals and can be seen working together to hunt schools of small fish. And, if you listen closely, you might even hear one singing.

10 Recording Gentle Giants

Marine biologist[2] Jim Darling has studied the songs of humpback whales for more than 25 years. While recording whale songs on a boat near Hawaii, he invited author Douglas Chadwick to experience diving with a humpback. In the water,

15 Chadwick heard the whale's songs in a way he never heard them before. "Suddenly, I no longer heard the whale's voice in my ears," he said. "I felt it inside my head and bones."

1 Someone or something that is **lighthearted** is cheerful and happy.

2 A **marine biologist** is a scientist who studies ocean life.

When swimming with the whale, Chadwick could see that the whale was **aware** of him, but not **alarmed** by his presence.

20 The 13-meter-long giant looked him over[3] **curiously**, but never harmed him. The whale then swam under the boat. It pointed its head down to the ocean floor and, with flippers[4] extended out to its sides, began to sing. Up in the boat, Darling recorded the whale's song. Humpback whale songs can be long and

25 **complex**, sometimes lasting for 30 minutes or more. They are perhaps the longest songs sung by any animal.

Why Do They Sing?

Darling says that only male humpbacks sing, but for **unknown** reasons. It was previously thought that they sang to attract

30 females, but scientists showed this was incorrect when they played recordings of whale songs in the ocean and the female whales did not respond. Another idea is that male humpbacks compete with each other using songs, just as other male animals on land do using their antlers or tusks.[5]

35 Researchers have also found that humpback whale songs are different in different parts of the world, perhaps like whale national anthems.[6] They may also be like hit tunes on the radio, changing over time—from one year to the next, or even over a **single** breeding **season**.

40 There is still so much the scientists don't know, and years of study lie ahead for whale researchers like Jim Darling. "Why do I do it?" he wonders aloud. "Human beings like puzzles. I want to know. Period."

Another member of the research team, photographer Flip

45 Nicklin, recalls a special moment he had while **interacting** with a humpback. While he was snorkeling some distance from the huge animal, it approached him until it was just a few meters away. It then gently carried Nicklin toward its eye with a flipper, as if examining him. **Apparently**, the urge to understand a

50 different species goes both ways.

---

3 If you **look** something **over**, you examine it for a short period of time.

4 **Flippers** are the two flat body parts that stick out from the side of a whale, seal, etc.

5 **Antlers** are long, branched horns that grow on the heads of some animals, like deer or moose; **tusks** are the long, pointed teeth of some animals, like walruses.

6 A **national anthem** is a country's song, chosen by a country's government to represent its people.

Long-distance travelers

Humpback whales make the longest migrations of
any mammal. Some travel over 4,000 kilometers
(2,500 miles) to find food in the summer.

Reading Comprehension

Multiple Choice. Choose the best answer for each question.

Gist

1. What is this reading mainly about?
   a. how to record humpbacks in the ocean
   b. how humpbacks communicate with people
   c. humpback songs and what they might mean
   d. the career of a man who is interested in humpbacks

Detail

2. When the scientists played whale songs in the ocean, _____.
   a. the songs attracted fish
   b. no female whales came
   c. male whales became angry
   d. male and female whales sang together

Detail

3. What is NOT true about humpback whales?
   a. Their songs are short and simple.
   b. Only male humpback whales sing.
   c. Their songs differ from place to place.
   d. They are popular with whale watchers.

Detail

4. The passage compares humpback songs to *hit tunes on the radio* because _____.
   a. the whales' songs are beautiful
   b. the whales sing songs very often
   c. the songs can last over 30 minutes
   d. the whales change their songs often

Did You Know?

The tail of each humpback has a different shape and different patterns. Researchers use these patterns to identify the whales they study.

Inference

5. In line 43, why does Darling say *Period*?
   a. to stress a long period of time
   b. to compare humans and puzzles
   c. to emphasize the previous sentence
   d. to let the listener know he plans to say more

Vocabulary

6. In line 49, the word *urge* could be replaced by _____.
   a. need   b. way
   c. difficulty   d. ability

Main Idea

7. What do Chadwick and Nicklin have in common?
   a. They were afraid of whales.
   b. They swam with the whales.
   c. Their jobs are to take photos of the whales.
   d. They are marine biologists studying whales.

Understanding Pronoun Reference

Writers use pronouns to refer to certain people or things. Pronouns allow a writer to avoid repeating the same nouns again and again. In the example below, the subject of the second sentence (*they*) refers to a noun in the first sentence (*humpback whales*).

Herman Melville . . . wrote that humpback whales were "the most lighthearted of all the whales." A favorite of whale watchers everywhere, <u>they</u> swim in ocean areas . . .

A pronoun usually, but not always, refers to something earlier in the sentence or in a previous sentence. The context should help you understand what the pronoun is referring to.

A. Reference. What does each <u>underlined</u> word refer to? Circle **a**, **b**, or **c**.

1. Humpbacks are known to be intelligent animals and can be seen working together to hunt schools of small fish. And, if you listen closely, you might even hear <u>one</u> singing.

    a. a humpback whale   b. an intelligent animal   c. a school of small fish

2. Marine biologist Jim Darling has studied the songs of humpback whales for more than 25 years. While recording whale songs on a boat near Hawaii, <u>he</u> invited author Douglas Chadwick to experience diving with a humpback.

    a. Jim Darling   b. Douglas Chadwick   c. the author

3. Humpback whale songs can be long and complex, sometimes lasting for 30 minutes or more. <u>They</u> are perhaps the longest songs sung by any animal.

    a. the researchers   b. humpback songs   c. male humpbacks

B. Reference. What does each **pronoun** from the reading refer to?

1. I felt **it** inside my head and bones. (line 17)   _____

2. The 13-meter-long giant looked **him** over . . . (line 20)   _____

3. **It** pointed its head down . . . (lines 21–22)   _____

4. **It** then gently carried Nicklin . . . (line 48)   _____

Critical Thinking Discuss with a partner. What reasons does the author give for the humpback whales' singing? What other reasons can you think of?

Vocabulary Practice

A. Completion. Complete the sentences using words from the box.
One word is extra.

| alarmed   apparently   aware   interact   leap   single |

1. Whales generally come up to breathe every 15 minutes, but some can hold their breath for up to an hour on a(n) _____ dive.

2. Many people are not _____ that many of the whales they see on whale-watching tours are later killed in areas where whaling is still allowed.

3. _____, there are some whale species that do not seem to migrate at all. They spend the entire year in one place.

4. Whales, sharks, and stingrays are animals that have been known to _____ from the water to catch their prey.

5. A whale-watching boat should move away from any whale that appears _____ by the boat's movements.

B. Definitions. Read the information. Then complete the definitions using the words in **red**.

Like humpbacks, blue whales sing **complex** songs. And like humpbacks, they are endangered. Fortunately, there are now laws that protect blue whales. Today, although their exact number is **unknown**, the blue whale population seems to be growing. Scientists are **curious** to know more about blue whale behavior, so they placed cameras on the whales. Through these cameras, it is possible to watch the whales as they swim, eat, and **interact** with each other. Using the whale cameras, scientists discovered that during breeding **season**, the females migrate to very food-rich areas to have their babies.

1. If something is _____, it has many parts and is difficult to understand.

2. A(n) _____ refers to a particular period of time during the year.

3. If something is _____, you have no knowledge of it.

4. When people or animals _____, they spend time together and communicate.

5. Someone who is _____ about something wants to learn or know more about it.

> **Thesaurus**
> **leap** Also look up:
> *(v.) jump, dive, soar, fly, hop, spring*

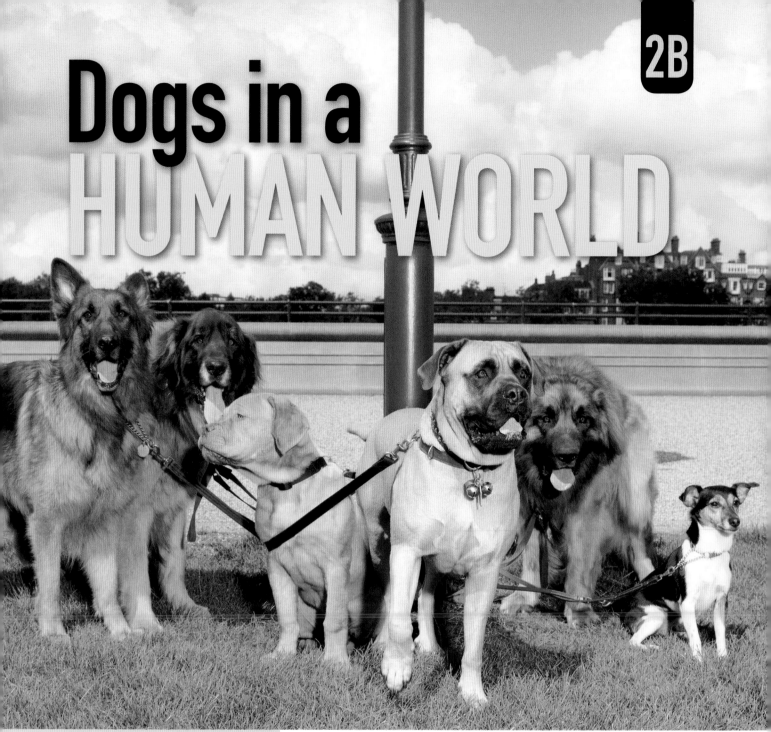

Dogs in a HUMAN WORLD

Before You Read

There are more than 300 different dog breeds on Earth. Each breed may have a unique look, but they are all members of one species, *Canis lupus familiaris*, the domestic dog.

A. Discussion. Look at the picture and answer the questions.

1. How many dog breeds in the picture can you name?
2. Do any of these dogs have special abilities?
3. Which of these dogs can help humans?
4. Which dogs do you think make the best pets? Why?

B. Scan. Scan the passage on pages 30–31 to find and circle the three dog breeds mentioned. According to the passage, what is each breed like?

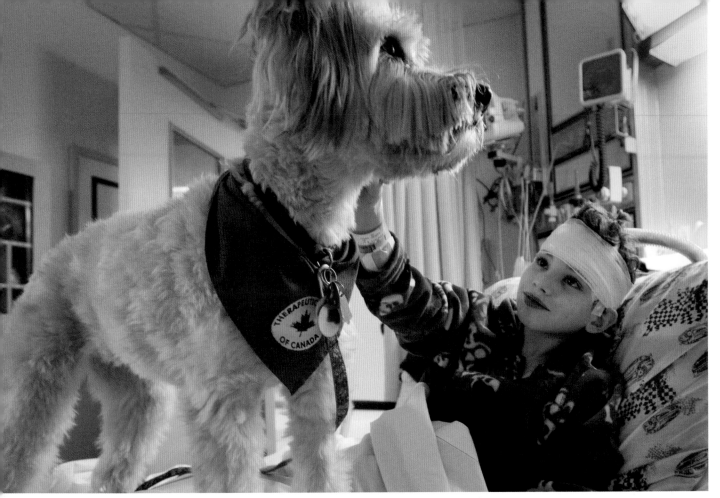

∧ Shaynee the therapy dog
visits children in the hospital.

Dogs and Humans

About 14,000 years ago, human beings and dogs began a
partnership that has lasted through the years. Our interactions may
have begun when wolves came close to our homes, attracted by
5 the smell of human **garbage**, or when humans found wolf puppies[1]
and trained them to be loving pets.

Today, by means of the careful **selection** of dog parents, humans
have created many different breeds of dog. Each breed has its own
look and **talents**, and its own role within human society. Here are
10 three examples of "a dog's life" in the human world.

The Animal Carer

Today, many hospitals let specially trained dogs in to bring love
and cheer to patients. Shaynee the wheaten terrier is a therapy
dog. She visits children who are fighting deadly diseases. Dogs like
15 Shaynee help patients feel calm and at peace, which can be hard
in a busy hospital. They help both children and adults stay strong
during long hospital stays, and, some suggest, even help them get
better.

1 **Puppies** are young dogs.

The Working Dog

20 Today, some beagles work in airports for the government. They are part of a program called the Beagle Brigade. A beagle is good for this type of work because of its powerful nose, and ability to **track** smells. The Beagle Brigade's job is to smell everything that comes into the country. They

25 alert officers to illegal fruits, vegetables, and other foods in **luggage** or in mail. The beagles do the job far better than any human could. Some of the dogs are **donated** by private owners; others were **rescued** from animal shelters.[2]

Toy dogs, like this Yorkshire terrier, make good pets for people who have small homes.

The Pampered Pet

30 While some dogs are working hard, others are free to spend their days resting and playing. Across the world, many pet dogs are treated like children. Many have their own rooms and all the things a dog could want. Some, like the

35 Yorkshire terrier pictured above, even have their own clothes. Many of these pampered[3] pets spend their days playing, learning to be **obedient**, or even going to yoga (or doga) classes. Their owners give them the best, and

40 enjoy doing so.

Whether as workers or objects of **affection**, dogs have become beneficial to humans in many ways. There are **plenty** of advantages for the dog, too. Many species of wild dogs

45 have nearly disappeared from the Earth. However, the domestic dog's special place as "man's best friend" has allowed it to survive in a human world.

---

2 An **animal shelter** is a place where animals that are lost or have no owners are kept.

3 If a person or an animal is **pampered**, they live a very comfortable life and are treated very well.

For centuries, humans have used beagles to help them hunt and track animals.

Reading Comprehension

Multiple Choice. Choose the best answer for each question.

Purpose

1. The author's purpose in writing is to _____.
   a. suggest that dogs be better cared for
   b. compare dogs to other helpful animals
   c. show examples of how dogs interact with humans
   d. show how dogs have not changed over many years

Vocabulary

2. In line 7, *by means of* could be replaced with _____.
   a. by the way
   b. as a result of
   c. knowing that
   d. on the other hand

Detail

3. According to the passage, beagles _____.
   a. can be dangerous
   b. can protect little children
   c. can bring people comfort
   d. are good at finding things

Detail

4. According to the passage, some pampered pets _____.
   a. eat human food   b. go to yoga class
   c. work for their owners   d. visit hospitals

Reference

5. In line 40, the phrase *doing so* refers to _____.
   a. training their dogs well
   b. taking their dogs to work
   c. looking after sick children
   d. treating their pets very well

Detail

6. What is true about Shaynee and members of the Beagle Brigade?
   a. They are working dogs.
   b. They visit children.
   c. They keep the country safe.
   d. They were rescued from a shelter.

Main Idea

7. What would be the best heading for the last paragraph?
   a. Dogs of Affection
   b. Benefits of Wild Dogs
   c. A Special Relationship
   d. Everyone Needs a Pet

Did You Know?

The first creature to go into space was a dog. In 1957, the Soviet Union sent a dog named Laika up in a rocket to circle the Earth.

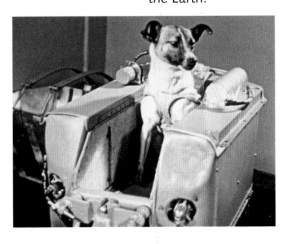

Scanning for Details

We scan a text to find specific information, such as a name, a date, a place, a number, or a reason. Decide what exactly you need to look for, and then quickly look only for that information. Do not read every word.

A. Scan. Read the questions below. For each question, decide what information you need to look for. Then scan the reading on pages 30–31 quickly to find the answers.

1. When did humans' partnership with dogs begin?

   (name / place / date / number / reason) **Answer:** _____

2. Who is a therapy dog?

   (name / place / date / number / reason) **Answer:** _____

3. Why do some hospitals let dogs in?

   (name / place / date / number / reason) **Answer:** _____

4. Where does the Beagle Brigade work?

   (name / place / date / number / reason) **Answer:** _____

5. What is dog yoga known as?

   (name / place / date / number / reason) **Answer:** _____

∨ Some dog breeds make good guide dogs. They help people find their way around.

B. Scan. Are these sentences true (**T**) or false (**F**)? Scan the reading and captions on pages 30–31 to find the information you need.

1. The first dogs that humans interacted with were wolves.   **T**   **F**
2. Therapy dogs help people in the hospital by bringing them food.   **T**   **F**
3. Some beagles in the Beagle Brigade were rescued from animal shelters.   **T**   **F**
4. Many species of wild dogs have nearly disappeared from the Earth.   **T**   **F**

Critical Thinking Discuss with a partner. Dogs are often called "man's best friend." Do you think it's true? What other animals have a close relationship with humans?

Vocabulary Practice

A. Matching. Read the information below. Then match each definition below with a word in **red**.

Dogs were probably first attracted to humans by the smell of our **garbage**. Today, some governments have found a use for those powerful noses that is beneficial to all who fly in airplanes. They train dogs to smell, **track**, and find bombs on planes and in **luggage**. The dogs are easy to train because they already have a deep connection to humans. Many of these dogs are **donated** to the program, where they can be given a good home. The partnership between dogs and humans allows each to profit from the special **talents** of the other as they work together to save lives.

1. _____: bags you carry when you travel
2. _____: trash, things you throw away
3. _____: to follow the path of something, to find its location
4. _____: given in order to help a person or an organization
5. _____: better than normal abilities, usually natural

B. Completion. Complete the information using the correct words from the box. One word is extra.

affection	garbage	obedient	plenty	rescue	select

Each breed of dog has its own role in our world. Some dog breeds, for example, can be trained to **1.** _____ people after an accident. Other breeds help protect our homes. People usually **2.** _____ breeds like German shepherds, rottweilers, and bull mastiffs to be guard dogs. These dogs can be fierce—and dangerous at times. If well-trained, however, they are **3.** _____ pets that can provide their owners with **4.** _____ of attention, as well as love and **5.** _____.

German shepherds are known for their strength and intelligence. They make good working dogs. >

> **Thesaurus**
> **talent** Also look up:
> *(n.) ability, aptitude, gift*

VIEWING Man's Best Friend

Before You Watch

A. Warm Up. Look at the picture below and read the caption. Then answer the questions.

∧ The husky is a breed of dog that is most at home in the cold temperatures of Siberia, in north Asia, and in the Arctic, where they have been helping humans hunt and travel for centuries. They can pull heavy sleds across the ice for great distances.

1. What breed of dog are these?

2. Where can you find these dogs?

3. How can these dogs help people?

While You Watch

A. Preview. Read the topics below. Then, while you watch, check (✓) the topics that are mentioned.

☐ examples of dogs that help humans

☐ a dog's sense of smell

☐ history of human partnership with dogs

☐ how to train a dog

☐ famous dogs from TV and movies

☐ theories on why humans acquired dogs

After You Watch

A. Multiple Choice. Circle the correct answer to each of the questions below.

1. Which breed of dog helps people herd livestock, like sheep?

   a. beagle   b. husky   c. border collie

2. A dog's sense of smell is _____ times more powerful than that of a human.

   a. 100   b. 1,000   c. 10,000

3. Which of these facts about wolves is NOT mentioned in the video?

   a. It's not easy to keep a wolf as a pet.
   b. Over the years, they became the pet we know today.
   c. Humans began working with wolves in the distant past.

4. Why did humans first train dogs to be pets?

   a. for hunting   b. for companionship   c. No one knows.

B. Matching. What else do you know about dog breeds? Match the dogs with the descriptions. Then check your answers at the bottom of the page.

1. _____: a very fast dog
2. _____: a very tall dog
3. _____: a very small dog
4. _____: a very smart dog
5. _____: a very fierce dog

d Irish wolfhound

c border collie

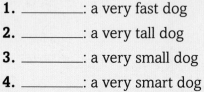

a German shepherd

b chihuahua

e greyhound

C. Discuss. Discuss these questions in a group. If you could choose any of the dogs described on pages 30–31 or in the video as a pet, which breed would you choose? Why?

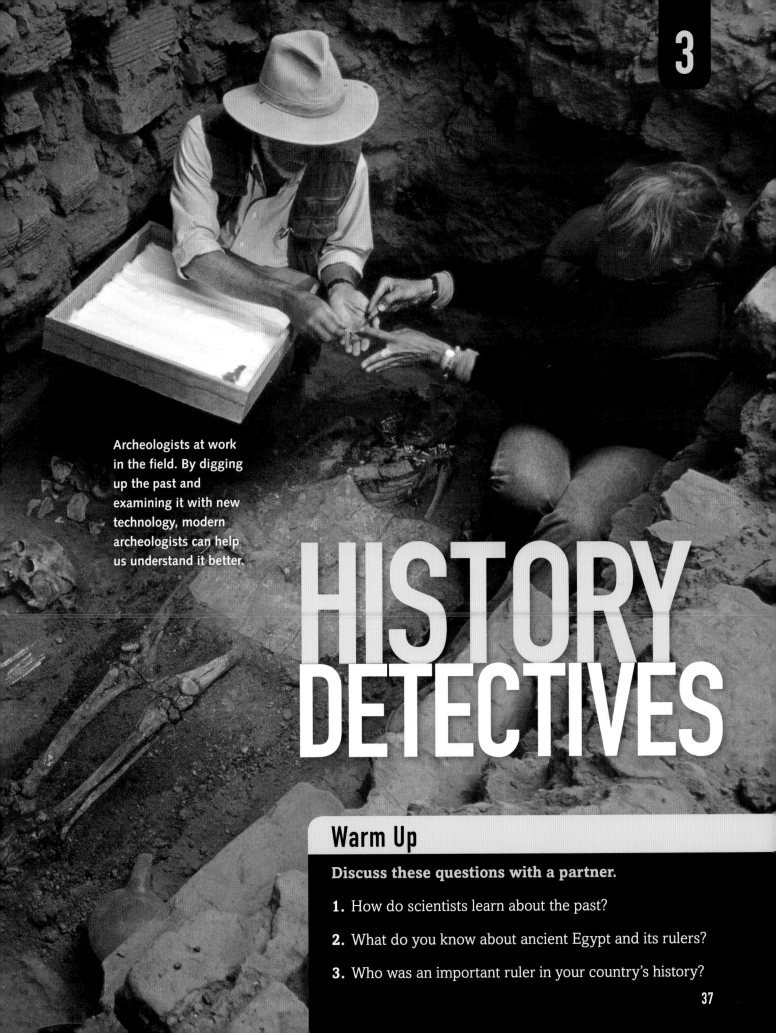

Archeologists at work in the field. By digging up the past and examining it with new technology, modern archeologists can help us understand it better.

3

HISTORY DETECTIVES

Warm Up

Discuss these questions with a partner.

1. How do scientists learn about the past?

2. What do you know about ancient Egypt and its rulers?

3. Who was an important ruler in your country's history?

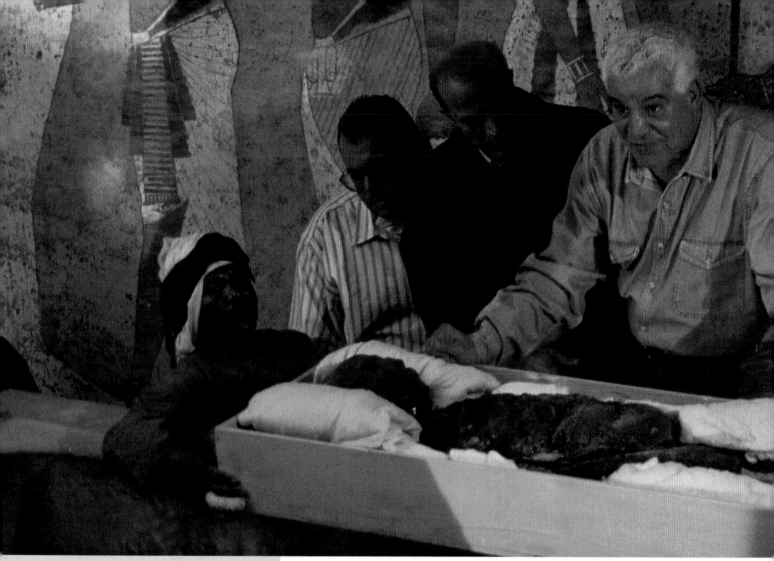

Before You Read

The all-Egyptian research team, led by Dr. Zahi Hawass (center), examines the mummy of King Tut, kept safely in Tut's richly painted tomb.

A. Completion. Look at the picture and read the information below. Match each word in **bold** with the correct definition.

On November 4, 1922, a British **archeologist** named Howard Carter discovered the **tomb** of King Tutankhamen. Inside, he found a beautiful solid gold **coffin** containing a **mummy.** It was the body of the young Egyptian king who had died over 3,200 years before.

1. archeologist •   • a. a preserved body

2. tomb •   • b. a room used to bury the dead

3. coffin •   • c. a box in which a dead body is kept

4. mummy •   • d. a scientist who studies things and people from the past

B. Scan. What are some theories about how King Tutankhamen died? Quickly scan the passage. Then compare your ideas with a partner.

Was King Tut Murdered?

An X-ray image of
King Tut's head, taken
by a CT scanner

1   At just 19 years old, King Tutankhamen was still a teenager when
he died in 1322 B.C. He ruled over all of Egypt for ten years, the last
king of a powerful family that had ruled Egypt for centuries. After
his death, the body of King Tut (as Tutankhamen is usually known
5   today) was placed in a **luxurious**, gold-filled tomb. There, he lay
forgotten until the tomb's eventual discovery in 1922. Although we
know a lot about his life, the reason for King Tut's death at such a
young age has remained a mystery, with **murder** the most extreme
possibility. Now, improved X-ray technology[1] and DNA[2] testing are
10   **offering** new clues into the life and death of the boy-king.

Discovered and Damaged

When British archeologist Howard Carter opened King Tut's tomb, it
was still full of gold and other amazing items. Carter spent months
carefully recording the treasures. When he and his team then
15   attempted to remove King Tut's mummy, they found that it had
become **attached** to its solid gold coffin. Unfortunately, they did a
great deal of damage to the mummy while removing it.

1 **X-ray technology** is a
special way of taking
pictures of the inside of
something.

2 **DNA** (deoxyribonucleic
acid) is the material that
carries information on how
a living thing will look or
function.

Theories about Tutankhamen's Death

In 1968, archeologists **conducted** an examination of King Tut's mummy using simple X-ray technology. Three important discoveries led to various theories about his death.

- The X-rays showed that bones in Tut's chest[3] were missing. Some guessed the damage was caused by a war **injury** or an accident.

- There was a small hole in the back of the skull, and pieces of bone inside it, causing many to believe that Tut was killed by a blow to the back of the head. Was he murdered by people wanting to take control of Egypt?

- A serious fracture was discovered on Tut's left leg. Tut was hurt a few hours before his death. This could have been the result of an accident. Could an infection from the injury have killed Tut?

A Closer Look

In 2005, scientists under the direction of Egyptian archeologist Zahi Hawass used new and more **effective** X-ray technology to study the mummy. They discovered that the damage to Tut's chest was caused by Howard Carter, and the hole in Tut's skull was made when embalmers[4] were preparing the body for burial. While this **ruled out** one theory, that of murder, it still doesn't tell us exactly how he died.

Then, in 2008, Hawass and his team **analyzed** Tut's DNA. They found that he suffered from flat feet as well as a bone disease that would have made it difficult for him to walk. When they analyzed the DNA of the mummies in other tombs nearby, they made some shocking discoveries. They found Tut's father and mother, who had similar DNA, were actually brother and sister. The DNA they passed on to Tut may have left him highly **vulnerable** to disease. Did an infection that started in his fractured leg—added to the bone disease—cause his death? No one knows for sure. But Hawass and his team hope they will someday have an answer to this age-old mystery.

⌄ Through CT scans of King Tut's mummy, scientists are learning more and more about how the boy-king lived and how he might have died.

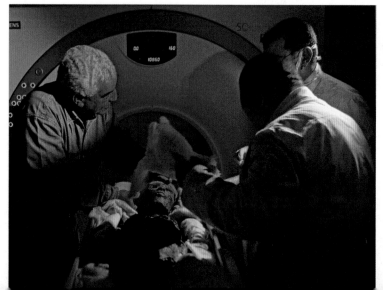

---

3 Your **chest** is the top part of the front of your body.

4 **Embalmers** are people who prepare a body for burial.

Inside King Tut's Tomb

The tomb of Tutankhamen was found hidden in the Valley of the Kings. Although some of its outer rooms were robbed in ancient times, the tomb itself was not opened. Inside were walls decorated with colorful paintings and nine layers of wood, stone, and gold, protecting the body of the king.

To reach King Tut's mummy, Carter and his team had to remove four huge boxes, or shrines. Each shrine was made from heavy wood and covered with golden pictures of the Egyptian gods.

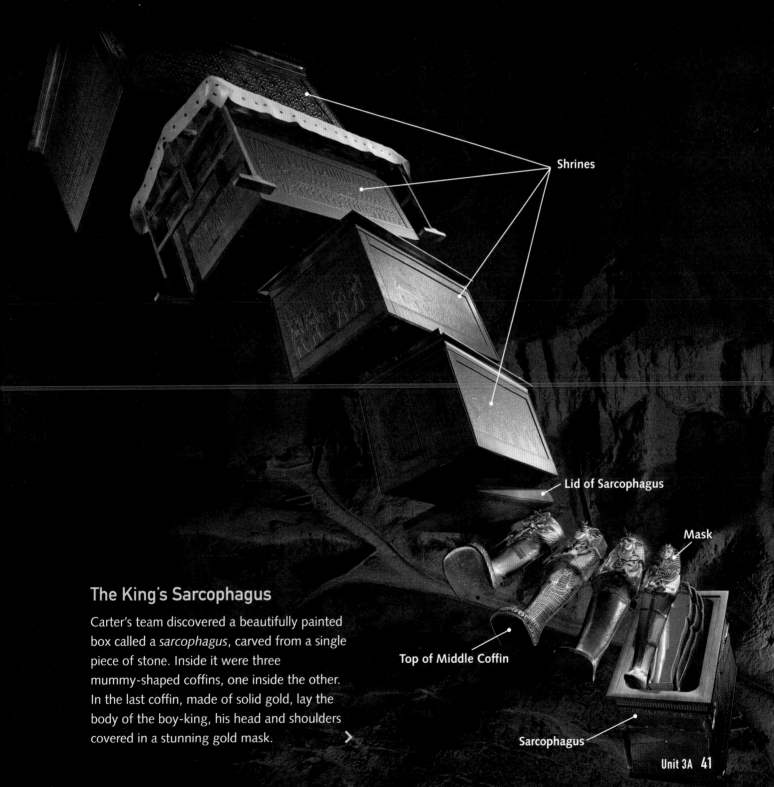

Shrines

Lid of Sarcophagus

Mask

Top of Middle Coffin

Sarcophagus

The King's Sarcophagus

Carter's team discovered a beautifully painted box called a *sarcophagus*, carved from a single piece of stone. Inside it were three mummy-shaped coffins, one inside the other. In the last coffin, made of solid gold, lay the body of the boy-king, his head and shoulders covered in a stunning gold mask.

Reading Comprehension

Multiple Choice. Choose the best answer for each question.

Gist

1. How does the passage answer the question, "Was King Tut murdered?"
   a. He was probably murdered.
   b. He almost certainly died in an accident.
   c. How he died is still not known.
   d. He died from a blow to the head.

Detail

2. Which of the following has NOT been suggested as a reason for King Tut's death?
   a. He died in an accident.   b. He was hit on the head.
   c. He died from an infection.   d. He was attacked by a snake.

Detail

3. How was King Tut's skull damaged?
   a. It was damaged during a war in Egypt.
   b. It was damaged by the new X-ray technology.
   c. It was damaged when it was removed from the coffin.
   d. It was damaged when the mummy was prepared for burial.

Vocabulary

4. In line 36, the phrase *ruled out* is closest in meaning to _____.
   a. suggested   b. confirmed
   c. questioned   d. rejected

Detail

5. Which of the following did Carter NOT find in Tut's tomb?
   a. colorful paintings
   b. a stone sarcophagus
   c. Tut's parents
   d. a golden mask

Detail

6. What did scientists discover by analyzing King Tut's DNA?
   a. He suffered from a bone disease.
   b. He had an infection in his leg.
   c. He had a brother and a sister.
   d. He had a broken leg at the time of his death.

Reference

7. What does the word *they* refer to in line 42?
   a. Hawass and his team
   b. King Tut's parents
   c. King Tut's children
   d. other mummies

Did You Know?

More than 130 canes and walking sticks were found inside King Tut's tomb. Many showed signs of use. This tells us Tut was not able to walk properly.

Creating a Timeline of Events

When you read a text that describes a series of events, it can be useful to place the events on a timeline. This provides you with a clear picture of the important events in the order they happened. A timeline can be used for events that occurred on specific dates, as well as for events that cover a period of time.

A. Noticing. Find and underline these events in the reading on pages 39–41.

a. King Tut's DNA is analyzed.
b. King Tut begins his rule of Egypt.
c. King Tut is placed in a gold-filled tomb.
d. Howard Carter discovers King Tut's tomb.
e. Outer rooms of King Tut's tomb are robbed.
f. King Tut's family, a series of powerful kings, ruled Egypt.
g. More effective X-ray technology is applied to the mummies.
h. Images of King Tut's mummy are taken with simple X-ray technology.

⌃ The golden mask of Tutankhamen

B. Labeling. Label the timeline below with the events above.

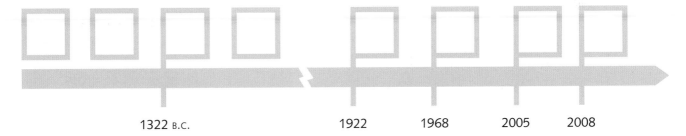

1322 B.C.   1922   1968   2005   2008

Critical Thinking Discuss with a partner. Do you think we'll learn how King Tut died someday? Is it important that we know how King Tut died? Why or why not?

Vocabulary Practice

A. Completion. Choose the correct words to complete the information.

Today, because of tests **1. (conducted / attached)** by researchers, we know a lot about ancient Egyptians through their mummies—for example, whether they died from illness or **2. (luxury / injury)**. We have also learned about people of the past through things buried with them. For example, the kings of ancient Egypt lived very **3. (vulnerable / luxurious)** lives. So when a tomb is found filled with treasure, archeologists can quickly **4. (rule out / murder)** the possibility that the tomb belonged to a poor person. Though ancient tombs are often very **5. (vulnerable / effective)** to grave robbing, many of the kings' tombs were hidden, so their treasures can tell us about how they lived.

B. Completion. Complete the information using the words from the box.

> analyze   attachment   effective   murder   offer

A group of mummies unearthed in South Korea may **1.** _____ hope for treating a deadly modern-day illness. They also tell of an ancient love story.

One of the bodies found shows signs that he was infected with the hepatitis B virus. Scientists hope that after they **2.** _____ the body, they will be able to better understand the disease, and find more **3.** _____ ways to treat it.

Another mummy was a young man who may have been involved in a plan to **4.** _____ the emperor. He was found buried with poems written by his wife. In the 500-year-old poems, she writes of her strong **5.** _____ to her husband, even beyond his death.

⌃ A mummy found in South Korea in 2007. A love poem buried with him reads:

I cannot live without you anymore.
I hope I could be with you.
Please let me go with you.
My love to you, it is unforgettable
in this world, and my sorrow,[1]
it is without end.

Thesaurus
effective Also look up: (*adj.*) *powerful, direct, useful, active, practical*

---

1 **Sorrow** is a feeling of extreme sadness.

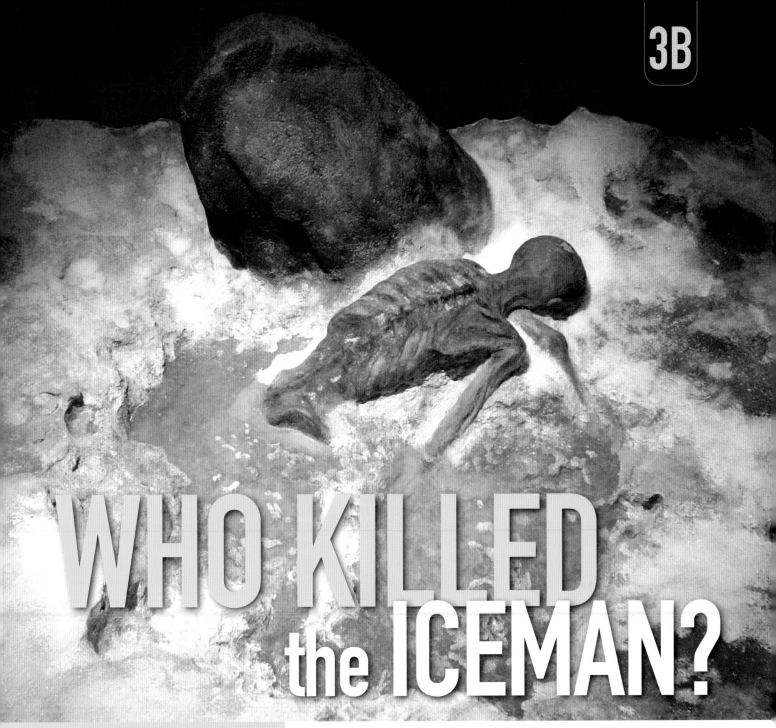

WHO KILLED the ICEMAN?

Before You Read

A model of the "Iceman," who was found frozen in the Alps

A. Discussion. A mummy, known as the "Iceman," was found high in the Alps in Italy in 1991. Look at the picture and read the caption. Then discuss the questions with a partner.

1. What kind of man do you think the "Iceman" was?

2. Where and when was he killed? What do you think happened to him?

B. Scan. Scan the reading passage on pages 46–47 to see if your predictions in **A** were correct.

DESCRIPTION OF BODY: **Male,** mid-forties. **Died** 5,300 years ago. **Possessions:** three layers of clothes, bearskin shoes, stone knife, copper ax, wooden arrows. **Condition:** deep cuts on hand and one on back, dark object visible under skin of left shoulder.

A Body in the Mountains

In 1991, high in the mountains of Europe, hikers made a gruesome[1] discovery: a dead man partly **frozen** in the ice. The police investigation soon became a scientific one. Carbon dating[2] **indicated** that the man died over 5,300 years ago. Today, he is known as the Iceman and nicknamed "Ötzi" for the Ötztal Alps where he was found. Kept in perfect condition by the ice, he is the oldest complete human body found on Earth.

Who Was the Iceman?

Scientists believe Ötzi was an important person in his society. Examinations of his teeth and skull tell us that he was not a young man. His arms were not the arms of a **laborer**. The things he carried also tell us about who he was. His knife was made of stone, but he carried a copper[3] ax. This was a valuable tool in Ötzi's time and **implies** that he was a **wealthy** man. A fire-starting kit was discovered with him, so we know he could make fire. And the food he ate and carried **enabled** scientists to **deduce** exactly where in Italy he lived—a village down in the valley.

Clues to an Ancient Murder

But why did Ötzi die in such a high and icy place? There have been many theories. Some said he was a lost shepherd.[4] Others thought he was killed in a religious ceremony. But these ideas were highly **debatable**.

Over the years, tiny scientific discoveries have led to great changes in our understanding of Ötzi's story. "[Once], the story was that he fled[5] up there and walked around in the snow and probably died of exposure,"[6] said scientist Klaus Oeggl. "Now it's all changed. . . . It's more like a . . . crime scene."

---

1 Something that is **gruesome** is unpleasant and shocking.
2 **Carbon dating** is a scientific method of finding out exactly how old an object is.
3 **Copper** is a soft, reddish brown metal.
4 A **shepherd** is a person whose job is to take care of sheep.
5 To **flee** means to escape.
6 **Exposure** is the harmful effect on your body from very cold weather.

A Bloody Discovery

In fact, the newest scientific information indicates Ötzi was **cruelly** murdered. In June 2001, an X-ray of the body showed a small dark shape **beneath** Ötzi's left shoulder. It was the stone head of 30 an arrow that had hit him from behind. CT scans showed that this caused an injury that killed him very quickly.

Then, in 2003, an Australian scientist discovered the blood of four other people on Ötzi's clothes. Was Ötzi killed in a bloody fight? It is unlikely, as Ötzi's other injuries, on his hand and head, had 35 already started to close. This may mean there had been a fight, but it happened much earlier.

Perhaps Ötzi was being chased when he died? In 2010, scientists took the mummy out of the cold and examined him again. They discovered that just before his death, he had a big meal of bread 40 and goat meat. Would someone being chased stop to eat a large meal? The scientists don't think so. More likely, he was attacked while resting. He may have thought he had escaped and was safe. Today, the research continues, proving some theories false while opening the door to others. Ötzi, it seems, has 45 more to tell us about his life and the time in which he lived.

In his last moments, the Iceman, Ötzi, lay in the cold, alone. There his body stayed for thousands of years.

Reading Comprehension

Multiple Choice. Choose the best answer for each question.

Gist

1. What is this reading mainly about?
   a. how people in the Italian Alps lived long ago
   b. what scientists have learned about an ancient death
   c. why mummies can last so long in the mountains
   d. why theories about the Iceman are often wrong

Inference

2. Why did the police stop investigating Ötzi's murder?
   a. They found his killer.
   b. It wasn't a recent murder.
   c. They needed the scientists' help.
   d. They couldn't find out why he died.

Detail

3. Why do scientists believe Ötzi was not a young man?
   a. His clothes were those of an older man.
   b. He was an important person in his society.
   c. His arms did not look very strong.
   d. His teeth and skull were those of an older man.

Reference

4. What does the word *it* in line 25 refer to?
   a. the story   b. the man
   c. the snow   d. the crime

Detail

5. What caused the death of the Iceman?
   a. an ax   b. a knife
   c. an arrow   d. the cold

Detail

6. Why is it believed that a fight took place long before Ötzi's death?
   a. The blood on his clothes was dry.
   b. He was bleeding from his shoulder.
   c. There were no weapons found on him.
   d. Injuries on his hand and head had begun to close.

Vocabulary

7. In line 44, what does *opening the door to* mean?
   a. allowing for the possibility of
   b. removing the chance of
   c. disproving the idea of
   d. providing a reason for

Did You Know?

The Iceman's body has the oldest blood cells ever found. They are so well preserved that they look like cells from a modern person.

Distinguishing Facts from Theories

Scientific and historical texts often contain a mix of both facts and theories. Facts are ideas that are known to be true, or can be proven. Theories are ideas that have not been proven to be true or false. Words that may indicate a theory include *think, believe, may, might, could, possibly, probably, perhaps,* and *(un)likely*. For example, the idea that Ötzi died over 5,300 years ago (line 5) is considered a fact, because it can be proven by carbon dating.

A. Noticing. Look back at the reading on pages 46–47. Find this information about Ötzi and underline it in the text.

  _**F**_   1. He was found in the mountains.

  _____   2. He died over 5,300 years ago.

  _____   3. He was an important person in his society.

  _____   4. Blood from four people was found on his clothes.

  _____   5. He had injuries on his hand and head.

  _____   6. A bloody fight took place before his murder.

  _____   7. He was being chased following a fight.

  _____   8. He had goat meat and bread before he died.

  _____   9. He was resting when he was attacked.

  _____ 10. He thought he was safe when he was attacked.

B. Fact or Theory. Which of the statements above are facts (**F**), and which are theories (**T**)? Write **F** or **T** next to each statement above. Then circle the words in the reading on pages 46–47 that indicate the theories.

Critical Thinking Discuss with a partner. How convinced are you that the Iceman was killed while resting? What other possible explanations for the Iceman's death can you think of?

⌃ The Iceman is hit in the shoulder by a stone arrow. Scientists believe this is what killed him.

Vocabulary Practice

A. Definitions. Read the information below. Then complete the definitions using the correct form of the words in **red**.

How did the Iceman last over 5,000 years? Scientists thought Ötzi's body may have dried out, like mummies in Egypt. However, Egyptian mummies still have hair. Ötzi's did not. This difference **enabled** scientists to **deduce** that the body had been preserved by a different process. Bodies that stay in water for a long time lose their hair. So, the fact that he had no hair **implies** that his body was underwater before it was **frozen** in the ice, although this is still **debatable**.

1. If something is _____, it is open to discussion or argument.

2. If you _____ something, you reach a conclusion because of other facts.

3. If something is _____, it has become very hard because of the cold.

4. If you _____ that something is true, you make others think that it is true.

5. If you _____ something to happen, you help to make it possible.

B. Completion. Complete the information with the correct words from the box. One word is extra.

> beneath   cruel   freeze   indicates   laborer   wealthy

1. Ötzi's _____ attackers left him to die in the cold.

2. In Ötzi's time, being _____ meant you had fine tools, warm clothing, a house, and animals.

3. Scientists believe that Ötzi was not a(n) _____ because his body doesn't show the damage caused by a life of hard work.

4. Evidence _____ that the cause of Ötzi's death was the arrowhead, only two centimeters across, found under his shoulder.

5. Ötzi's mummy was buried _____ the ice and snow for thousands of years.

Word Partnership
Use **debate** with: (*adj.*) **open to** debate, **major** debate, **political** debate, **presidential** debate; (*v.*) debate **over something**, debate **the issue**.

VIEWING Inca Mummy

Before You Watch

^ In 1995, archeologist Johan Reinhard found the mummy of a young girl on a frozen
peak in the Andes mountains in Peru. Unlike Ötzi, she had been carefully placed in a
unique burial site. The scientists named her "Juanita," after Reinhard.

A. Preview. These words are from the video. Match each word to its definition.

1. blow   •   • a. a powerful stroke with a hand or hard object

2. burial   •   • b. the top of a mountain

3. peak   •   • c. the act of putting someone in the ground

4. sacrifice   •   • d. the killing of an animal or a person in a religious
                           ceremony

B. Predict. Look at the picture above and read the caption. How do you think
Juanita died? Circle **a**, **b**, **c**, or **d**. Then watch the video to check your prediction.

a. She was buried alive.   b. She was hit on the head.

c. She froze to death.   d. She fell off a mountain peak.

While You Watch

A. Number these events from 1 to 4 in the order they occurred.

☐ The archeologists remove some pots from the ground.

☐ The body of a mummified Inca girl was found.

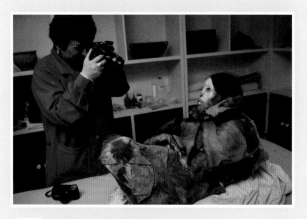

☐ Scientists deduce the cause of the Inca girl's death.

☐ Two bodies are discovered under a pattern of stone circles.

After You Watch

A. Fact or Theory. Which of the statements below are facts (**F**) and which are theories (**T**)?

1. _____ The Quechuan are direct descendants of the Inca people.

2. _____ The Incas sacrificed Juanita because they believed it would make the mountain gods treat them well.

3. _____ The six stone circles showed the location of some burial sites.

4. _____ The skull injury that Juanita received ended her life.

B. Discuss. Discuss these questions in a group.

1. What do you think helped preserve the mummies in the video?

2. What can these mummies teach scientists about the ancient Inca people?

3. How is Juanita different from the mummies of King Tut and Ötzi?

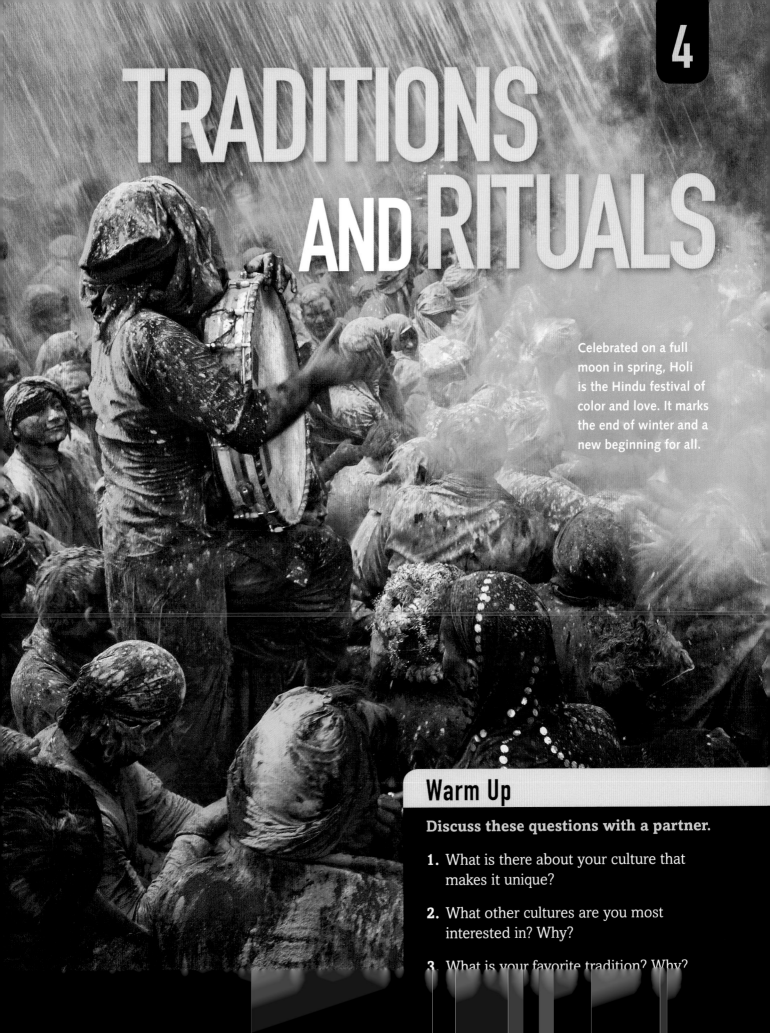

4

TRADITIONS AND RITUALS

Celebrated on a full moon in spring, Holi is the Hindu festival of color and love. It marks the end of winter and a new beginning for all.

Warm Up

Discuss these questions with a partner.

1. What is there about your culture that makes it unique?

2. What other cultures are you most interested in? Why?

3. What is your favorite tradition? Why?

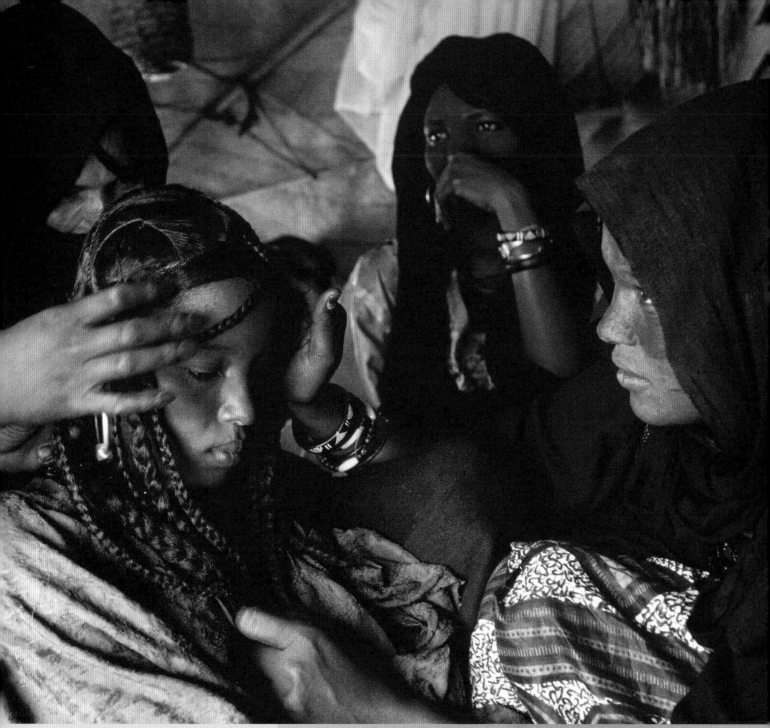

Assalama, a young Tuareg bride, prepares for a big celebration with the help of her relatives.

Before You Read

A. Discuss. Look at the title, photo, and caption. What celebration do you think Assalama is getting ready for?

B. Skimming for the Main Idea. What do you think the reading on page 55 is mainly about? Circle **a**, **b**, or **c**. Then read the passage to check your answer.

a. a famous African bride

b. a traditional wedding

c. traditional desert clothing

BRIDE OF THE SAHARA

1　The Tuareg bride, Assalama, sits silently as relatives and helpers make sure her hair is perfect for the **wedding**. Such attention is new for the bride, who is only 15 years old and has spent most of her life taking care of her family's goats and sheep. The Tuareg are nomads,[1] and it was only by chance that she was

5　**reunited** with her 25-year-old cousin Mohamed a month earlier. Back from working in Libya, Mohamed spotted Assalama as she drew water from a well. "I knew from that moment that I wanted to marry her," he says. He asked for her hand and she said "yes," giving him a piece of jewelry to **demonstrate** her acceptance. Their families **approved**, and wedding plans began.

10　Following Tuareg traditions, the marriage **ceremony** is performed at a mosque[2] in the presence of only the couple's parents. Assalama and Mohamed are absent. A few days later, the celebration begins. For a week, some 500 guests enjoy camel races, sing, and eat rice, dates, and roasted meat in **tents** under the Saharan stars.

15　Mohamed wears an indigo *tagelmust*, a cloth that **wraps** his head and face. The rich color, which rubs off onto the skin, earned these Saharan warriors[3] the title "blue men of the desert." For the Tuareg, the tagelmust not only keeps out sand and sun, it keeps evil[4] creatures called *jinns* away, as does *henna*, a reddish brown coloring used on Mohamed's feet. It is also a **symbol**

20　of purity, **reserved** for a man's first marriage.

A tent called an *ehan* is prepared for Assalama and Mohamed. Women take down and put up the marriage tent each day, making it larger each time. The growing tent symbolizes the couple's growing relationship. Through the whole celebration, Assalama stays inside the tent. She shows her face or

25　speaks only to Mohamed, her best friend, her mother, and one special helper. Assalama and Mohamed are never left alone, for fear they might be harmed by **jealous** jinns.

The couple will spend their first year of marriage with Assalama's family. Mohamed must work hard to win his in-laws' approval. Once he does

30　that, he will take his bride back to his camp and start his nomad's caravan moving again.

---

1 **Nomads** are people who don't live in one place. Instead, they move from place to place.

2 A **mosque** is a place where Muslims go to worship.

3 A **warrior** is a skilled fighter or a soldier.

4 Someone who is **evil** is very bad and causes harm to other people.

Reading Comprehension

Multiple Choice. Choose the best answer for each question.

Gist

1. What is the passage mainly about?
   a. the love story of two Tuareg cousins
   b. the changing festivals of the Tuareg people
   c. a description of the marriage of a Tuareg couple
   d. the marriage difficulties of a young Tuareg couple

Vocabulary

2. In lines 7–8, what does *he asked for her hand* mean?
   a. He asked her for some help.
   b. He asked her to hold hands.
   c. He asked her to marry him.
   d. He asked his parents for permission to marry.

Detail

3. During their actual marriage ceremony, Assalama and Mohamed _____.
   a. were not present
   b. visited a nearby mosque
   c. showed respect to their parents
   d. wore traditional Tuareg clothing

Did You Know?

The Tuareg depend on camels for transportation across the desert. Camels can drink up to 150 liters of water at a time, and have been known to survive 50 days without water.

Inference

4. Henna is used on Mohamed's feet because he _____.
   a. is marrying a cousin
   b. is not wearing a tagelmust
   c. is thought to be very pure
   d. has not been married before

Detail

5. Why was the marriage tent made larger and larger?
   a. because the celebration increases in size
   b. to chase jealous jinns further and further away
   c. to show the progress of the couple's relationship
   d. so Assalama's friend, mother, and helper could enter

Cause and Effect

6. The people are afraid that if Assalama or Mohamed are left alone, they will _____.
   a. turn into jealous jinns
   b. be harmed by evil creatures
   c. become jealous of other people
   d. change their minds about getting married

Reference

7. The word *that* in line 30 refers to Mohamed _____.
   a. returning to his camp
   b. winning his in-laws' approval
   c. starting his caravan moving again
   d. finishing the wedding celebration

Reading Skill

Dealing with Unfamiliar Vocabulary

A reading text can help readers understand vocabulary in a variety of ways. A word (often in a caption) may simply be shown in a photo, or a word may be defined immediately before or after it appears in the text. Look for a definition set off by commas, or for words like *means*, *is called*, or *known as*. At other times, a word might simply be defined at the end of the reading or in a footnote.

If a word is not shown or defined, it may still be possible to understand its meaning from context. Look at the words around it, and see if you can guess the meaning or have a general idea of its meaning.

A. Scan. These words appear in the passage on page 55. Find and circle them.

drew   ehan   henna   jinns   nomad   tagelmust   warrior

B. Matching. Use the context to help you identify the meaning of the words in **A**. Then match each of the words with its definition.

1. drew   •   • a. pulled up
2. nomad   •   • b. evil creatures
3. jinns   •   • c. a special type of tent
4. ehan   •   • d. a reddish brown coloring
5. tagelmust   •   • e. a type of fighter or soldier
6. warrior   •   • f. a cloth that wraps a head and face
7. henna   •   • g. a person who travels from place to place

A Tuareg man wears a traditional head-cloth called a *tagelmust*.

Critical Thinking Discuss with a partner. Do you think Mohamed and Assalama are the right age to get married? What is the ideal age to get married in your culture? Give reasons to support your opinions.

Vocabulary Practice

A. Completion. Complete the information below using the words from the box. One word is extra.

ceremony	jealous	reserved	reunite
symbolize	tents	weddings	wrap

Like the Tuareg, the Wodaabe are a group of nomadic African people who live in light **1.** _____ that can be moved from place to place. The Wodaabe never stay still for long, but do come together a few times a year for big celebrations. A special place is always **2.** _____ for guests.

Two important Wodaabe celebrations have to do with love. In the *geerewol* **3.** _____, young women choose a man to marry in a unique beauty contest. Wodaabe men **4.** _____ their heads in attractive turbans, and wear beads and shells that **5.** _____ wealth. They present themselves to the women, hoping to find a bride. Then, at the *worso* celebration, thousands of Wodaabe families **6.** _____ once again. They meet to celebrate all the **7.** _____ that have taken place in the past year!

∧ Beauty is very important to the Wodaabe. In the geerewol, the men wear makeup to show off their looks.

B. Completion. Complete the sentences using the correct form of the words in **red** on page 55.

1. If someone is _____ of another person, they want something the other person has.

2. If something is _____, it is kept for a particular purpose.

3. When people _____, they meet again after being separated.

4. A(n) _____ is a formal event, such as a wedding.

5. When you _____ something, you make it clear to other people.

6. If you _____ of something, you think it is good.

> **Word Link Re-** is added to verbs and nouns to make new verbs and nouns that refer to repeating an action or process. For example, *reread* means "read again," and someone's *re-election* is their being elected again.

The Changing Face of Kung Fu

Before You Read

A. Completion. Read the caption. Then complete the sentences below using the correct form of the words in **bold**.

1. A(n) _____ is a member of a male religious community.

2. _____ are skillful, athletic body movements such as jumping, spinning, rolling, etc.

3. A(n) _____ is a building for the practice of a religion.

4. If you are a(n) _____ of something, you know how to do it very, very well.

5. A(n) _____ is a formal style of hand-to-hand fighting, also often practiced as a sport.

B. Predict. The title of the reading is "The Changing Face of Kung Fu." How do you think kung fu today is different from kung fu in the past? Read the passage to check your ideas.

The Shaolin **Temple** has stood in the mountains of China's Henan Province for over 1,500 years. The **monks** who live there are **masters** of a **martial art** called kung fu. In movies, kung fu involves lots of **acrobatics**, which is not taught in more traditional styles of kung fu.

The Birthplace of Kung Fu

According to legend, in the fifth century, an Indian master taught some monks at the Shaolin Temple a **series** of exercises, or forms, **inspired** by the movements of animals. These forms
5 became the **basis** for the style of fighting known as kung fu. Over 16 centuries, the monks have used kung fu for **self-defense** and in war. With it, they have won many battles against their enemies.

In Dengfeng today, ten kilometers (six miles) from the Shaolin
10 Temple, there are over 60 martial arts schools with more than 50,000 students. Students come to the schools for a variety of reasons. Some hope to become movie stars. Others come to learn skills that will **ensure** good jobs in the military or police force. A few are sent by their parents to learn self-control and
15 hard work.

Master Hu Zhengsheng teaches at a small school in Dengfeng. Recently, he was offered an important role in a kung fu movie. It would have been good **publicity** for his school. However, he did not **accept**. He doesn't agree with how kung fu is often
20 shown in movies. He feels they show too much **violence**.

A young kung fu student demonstrates the skill with which he can bend his body.

At the Shaolin Temple, students as young as three or four years old can begin lessons in kung fu.

Unlike many large schools, which teach acrobatics and kickboxing, Hu teaches his students traditional kung fu forms. He teaches them the way his master—a Shaolin legend—taught him. But attracting new students to this style of kung fu has become a problem. Hu is afraid his art will soon die out.
25 He has to **remind** his students that kung fu was designed for fighting, not to entertain.

"There are no high kicks or acrobatics [here]," he says. "It is hard to **convince** boys to spend many years learning something that won't make them wealthy or famous."

30 Hu's students have little. They sleep in unheated rooms and train outside no matter what the temperature. They hit trees with their bare hands and take turns sitting on each other's shoulders to build leg strength. Why such hardship? To master kung fu, they must learn respect, and how to "eat bitterness," a Mandarin expression meaning "to endure suffering." The life
35 of a Shaolin master, Hu teaches, is not easy or attractive.

Master Hu is in a difficult position. For old traditions to survive, the young must learn. Gradually, he has begun offering a few courses in kickboxing and the acrobatic kung fu forms, hoping to attract new students. Then, maybe, he'll be able to convince them to learn Shaolin kung fu the traditional way.

Reading Comprehension

Multiple Choice. Choose the best answer for each question.

Gist

1. Why does the passage mention Hu Zhengsheng?
   a. He is a kung fu student learning kickboxing.
   b. He is the man who introduced kung fu to China.
   c. He is a kung fu master preserving old traditions.
   d. He is a famous actor in an exciting kung fu movie.

Detail

2. What is true about kung fu?
   a. It's over 17 centuries old.
   b. It was traditionally used for fighting.
   c. It was introduced to China from Thailand.
   d. It was originally designed to entertain people.

Detail

3. Which is NOT given as a reason why people study kung fu?
   a. to learn self-control
   b. to think more clearly
   c. to help get good jobs
   d. to become movie stars

Purpose

4. What is the purpose of the third paragraph?
   a. to show why Hu teaches acrobatics and kickboxing
   b. to convince people that they can be rich and famous
   c. to explain the challenges traditional kung fu schools face
   d. to show how Hu's ideas about kung fu are different from other kung fu teachers

Reference

5. What does *here* refer to in line 27?
   a. in kung fu movies   b. in the Shaolin Temple
   c. in Master Hu's school   d. in the city of Dengfeng

Paraphrase

6. Which of the following is closest in meaning to *no matter what the temperature* (line 31)?
   a. even if they feel sick
   b. even if it's very hot or cold
   c. only when the temperature is hot
   d. because it's warmer than in their rooms

Vocabulary

7. In line 34, the words *endure suffering* mean _____.
   a. stop the suffering   b. make someone suffer
   c. survive the suffering   d. make the suffering worse

Did You Know?

The term *kung fu* actually means "skill achieved through hard work" and can refer to a great skill in any area. Here, a Shaolin monk shows off his amazing soccer skills.

Differentiating Between Main Ideas and Supporting Details

A paragraph has one main idea. This is the most important piece of information that the author wants to put forward. It can be found in the topic sentence, usually (but not always) at or near the beginning of a paragraph. To determine the main idea, ask yourself, "What is this paragraph mainly about?" or "What point is the author trying to make?"

A paragraph is developed around this main idea. Supporting sentences may present facts, give reasons, make comparisons or contrasts, and provide examples, definitions, or details.

A. Main Ideas vs. Details. Look back at the reading on pages 60–61. In each pair of sentences from the reading below, identify the main idea (**M**) of the paragraph and the supporting sentence (**S**).

Paragraph 1
a. __S__ With it, they have won many battles against their enemies.
b. __M__ These forms became the basis for the style of fighting known as kung fu.

Paragraph 2
a. ___ Students come to the schools for a variety of reasons.
b. ___ Some hope to become movie stars.

Paragraph 3
a. ___ He feels they (movies) show too much violence.
b. ___ He doesn't agree with how kung fu is often shown in movies.

Paragraph 4
a. ___ He has to remind his students that kung fu was designed for fighting, not to entertain.
b. ___ Unlike many large schools, which teach acrobatics and kickboxing, Hu teaches his students traditional kung fu forms.

Paragraph 6
a. ___ Hu's students have little.
b. ___ The life of a Shaolin master, Hu teaches, is not easy or attractive.

Critical Thinking Discuss with a partner. What are some traditional practices in your country that are changing? Are the changes for the better? Why or why not?

Vocabulary Practice

A. Completion. Complete the information below using the words in the box.

> basis   convinced   ensure   inspired   series

Many kung fu forms have their **1.** _____ in the movements of animals, like the snake, crane, or tiger. Some were even **2.** _____ by the dragon, a mythical creature. These animals were admired for their fighting abilities. So the monks studied their habits—how they rested, hunted, and fought. The monks created a **3.** _____ of animal-like fighting styles.

According to Shaolin legend, as some monks studied an animal, they became **4.** _____ that they were like that animal. So the monks were not allowed to train in any one animal style for too long. Instead, they had to train in all the five styles so that each animal's strengths would be added to their own skills. To focus too much on one animal would **5.** _____ that a student became weaker, not stronger.

∧ Another animal style of kung fu is based on the movements of the praying mantis.

B. Words in Context. Complete each sentence with the correct answer.

1. You **remind** yourself to do something, so you _____ to do it.
   a. don't forget   b. can learn how

2. One way to **accept** someone's offer to do something is to say, "_____."
   a. Yes, please   b. No, thank you

3. **Violence** is behavior that is meant to _____.
   a. calm and relax   b. hurt or kill

4. Someone who wants **publicity** wants to _____ the public's attention.
   a. attract   b. avoid

5. A _____ is designed for **self-defense**.
   a. martial art   b. mirror

> **Word Link**
> The prefix **en-** means "make or cause to" and can be added to some adjectives to make them verbs, e.g., *ensure, enlarge, enrich, enslave.*

VIEWING Aboriginal Rock Art

Before You Watch

A. Definitions. Look at the picture and read the caption. Then match each word in **bold** with its definition.

❮ There are many places in the **outback** of Australia that are of great importance to the **Aborigines**. Some of these **sites** contain ancient rock paintings that tell stories of gods and ancient **spirits**. These paintings tell stories like that of the Rainbow **Serpent**, which is believed to protect the land.

1. _____ : a snake
2. _____ : the people who were living in Australia before Europeans
3. _____ : places that are used for a particular purpose
4. _____ : supernatural beings; forces within people that are believed to give their bodies life
5. _____ : the part of Australia that is far from towns and cities

While You Watch

A. True or False. Read the statements below. As you watch the video, mark each sentence as true (**T**) or false (**F**).

1. The rock art paintings in Australia are older than the pyramids of Egypt.   T   F
2. Aborigines settled in Australia about 25,000 years ago.   T   F
3. Some rock art paintings show something known as the Dreaming.   T   F
4. More and more older people know about the ancient stories.   T   F

After You Watch

A. Completion. Circle the correct word or phrase to complete each sentence.

1. These ancient sites were discovered (**only recently / a long time ago**).

2. The Dreaming describes the creation of rivers, mountains, and (**humans / gods**).

3. Aborigines believe that the Rainbow Serpent was the (**father / creator**) of everything we see.

4. The legends of the Dreaming have been (**lost in / passed down through**) time.

B. Discuss. Discuss these questions with a partner.

1. What stories have you heard from your elders, such as your grandparents?

2. Aboriginal elder Margaret Katherine says, "Don't forget your culture, and live on with it forever in your heart and mind." What do you think she means? What are some ways we can preserve a culture?

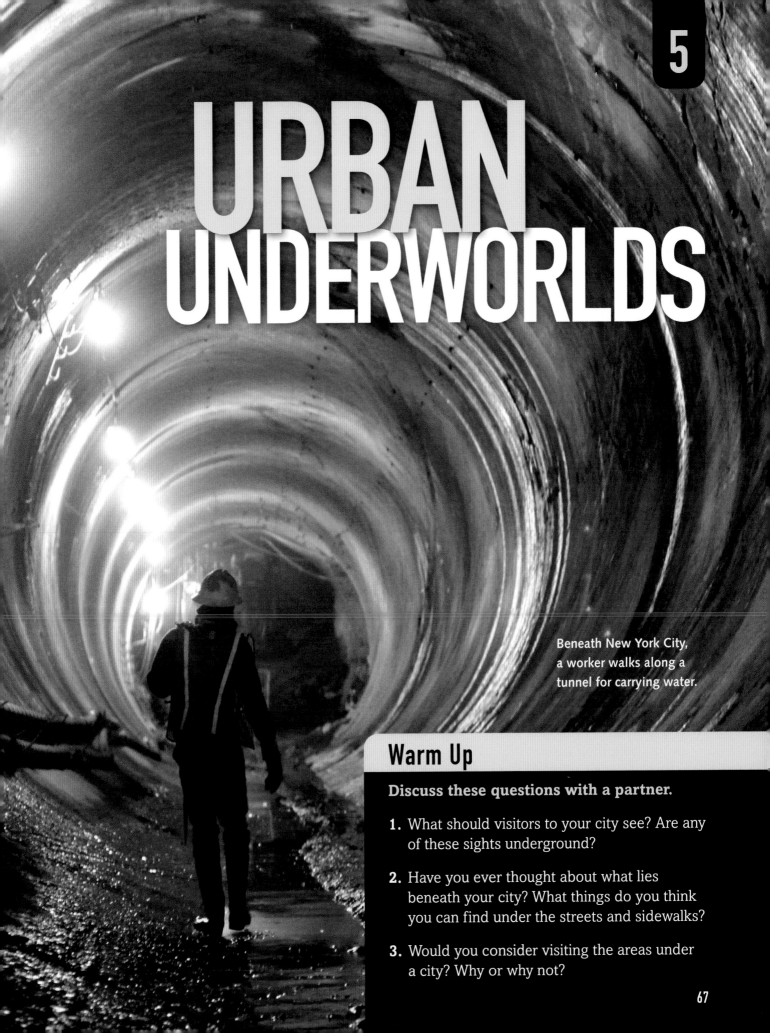

5

URBAN UNDERWORLDS

Beneath New York City, a worker walks along a tunnel for carrying water.

Warm Up

Discuss these questions with a partner.

1. What should visitors to your city see? Are any of these sights underground?

2. Have you ever thought about what lies beneath your city? What things do you think you can find under the streets and sidewalks?

3. Would you consider visiting the areas under a city? Why or why not?

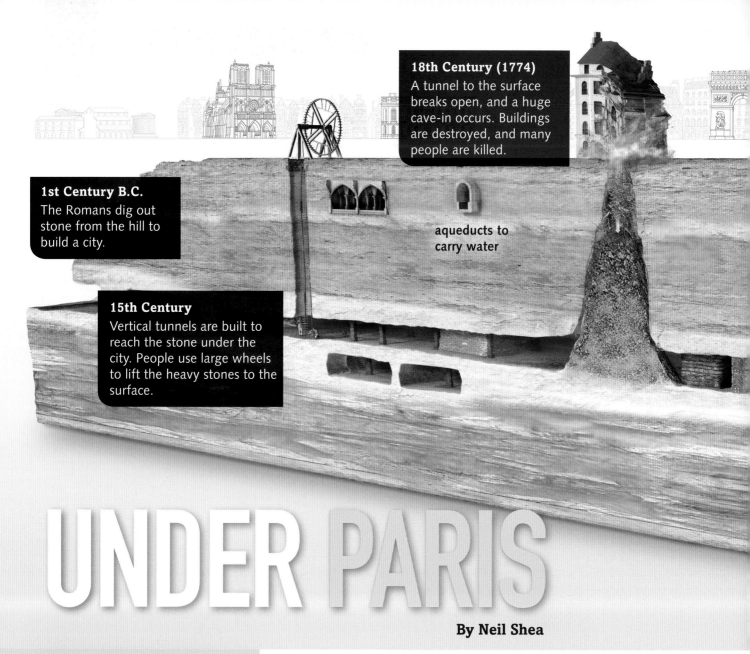

18th Century (1774)
A tunnel to the surface breaks open, and a huge cave-in occurs. Buildings are destroyed, and many people are killed.

1st Century B.C.
The Romans dig out stone from the hill to build a city.

aqueducts to carry water

15th Century
Vertical tunnels are built to reach the stone under the city. People use large wheels to lift the heavy stones to the surface.

UNDER PARIS

By Neil Shea

Before You Read

A. Matching. Look at the diagram of Paris above. Then match the events with the dates.

1. A cave-in swallowed buildings and people.　•　• a. 1800s
2. Paris's subway system, the Métro, was opened.　•　• b. 15th century
3. The sewers were improved and expanded.　•　• c. 1774
4. Wheels were used to lift stones to the surface.　•　• d. 1786
5. Bones were first poured into the tunnels.　•　• e. 1900

B. Scan. Though most of the tunnels beneath Paris are closed to the public, some urban explorers, known as *cataphiles*, still find their way into the tunnels. What do you think the cataphiles do underneath Paris? Scan the reading to find three things. Then read the whole passage.

19th Century (1800s)
To help keep the city clean, the sewers are improved and made bigger.

20th Century (1900)
Paris opens its first subway, the Métro. The earliest lines run close to the surface. Later subway systems would take people deeper underground and further out of the city.

sewers

utilities

Early Métro line

Present day Métro line

18th Century (1786)
With a growing city, and little space for the dead, millions of bones are poured into the tunnels.

WW2 bunker

Subway out of the city

1　I'm standing on a sidewalk in the early morning. The great avenues of Paris are **silent**, and the shops are closed. From a bakery comes the smell of fresh bread. Suddenly, a man with long hair and a lamp on his head appears from a hole in the sidewalk. He is soon
5　followed by a young woman holding a lantern.[1] Mud covers their boots. The man places the **iron** cover over the hole and takes the woman's hand. Together, they run down the street, smiling.

　　The couple had been exploring the **tunnels** beneath the city. When the Romans **occupied** Paris, they cut out stone from deep
10　within the earth to build their city and make **sculptures**. Later, the French used more stone to construct the Notre Dame Cathedral, the Louvre, and many other buildings. This left huge underground tunnels upon which part of the city now stands. Once used for

Like the famous city above, the Paris underground has grown over the centuries. Today, it is made up of over 300 kilometers of tunnels.

1　A **lantern** is a lamp in a metal frame with a handle on top so you can carry it.

growing mushrooms, burying the dead, or as hiding places during wartime, today they are mostly forgotten, except by "cataphiles"— people who love to go down into the tunnels below Paris, even though it's actually not **permitted**.

Paris, France

A City Rediscovered

Exploring the underground city first became a **trend** in the 1970s and '80s. It was easier to enter the tunnels then, because there were many more open **entrances** through forgotten doorways and into catacombs—rooms filled with bones. The bones had been moved into the tunnels to solve the problem of crowded cemeteries. By the end of the 1980s, most of the entrances were shut, and police regularly walked the tunnels. However, there are still cataphiles, like the couple I saw that morning, and for those who **dare**, the underground is an exciting place to meet, have parties, perform for each other, or create art.

A cataphile walks down a dark, flooded tunnel with only lantern-light to help him find his way.

Underground Explorations

30 My own exploration began beneath the old Paris opera house, where sewer² workers showed me a 55-meter-long underground pond, a pond that actually had fish in it! Later, at France's national bank, officials guided me below to an amazing room filled with 2,600 tons of gold.

35 As cataphiles are the best guides, I then asked Dominique and Yopie, experienced cataphiles, to give me a tour. **Descending** into the underground through a secret entrance beneath a bridge, we walked for hours through catacombs and galleries of huge, bright paintings. Yopie dove into water-filled passages to see where they
40 led. We stopped to rest in a room with stone furniture, where Yopie told me, "Many people come down here to party, some to paint. Some people to destroy or to create or to explore. We do what we want here. We don't have rules . . ."

---

2 A **sewer** is a large underground channel that carries waste matter and rain water away.

∨ In an area known as "the beach," cataphiles cover the walls with art, including a wave painted in the style of Japanese printmaker Hokusai.

Reading Comprehension

Multiple Choice. Choose the best answer for each question.

Gist

1. What is the reading mainly about?
a. why tourists know so little about Paris's tunnels
b. the tunnels under Paris and the people who explore them
c. why tunnels will someday be Paris's newest tourist attraction
d. how the recent discovery of Paris's tunnels is changing the city

Inference

2. Why was the couple that the writer met smiling as they ran down the street?
a. They were able to replace the iron cover.
b. They had discovered a dangerous tunnel below.
c. They had explored a tunnel without getting caught.
d. They felt dirty and wanted to run home and take a shower.

Detail

3. Which statement is NOT true about the tunnels under Paris?
a. People grew mushrooms there.
b. They were once used as a hiding place.
c. People explore them even though it's not permitted.
d. Companies remove the stone to construct modern buildings.

Detail

4. Why did it use to be easier to enter the tunnels?
a. The tunnels were safer.
b. There were more open entrances.
c. There was less water in the tunnels.
d. There were fewer dangerous people living there.

Purpose

5. What is the purpose of the fourth paragraph?
a. to give a personal account of visiting the tunnels
b. to describe how the tunnels were used in past decades
c. to give reasons why cataphiles should be hired as guides
d. to describe how the tunnels will likely be used in the future

Did You Know?

In certain parts of Paris, tall buildings cannot be built because the earth beneath is filled with tunnels and catacombs.

Reference

6. In line 41, what does the word *here* refer to?
a. the entrances   b. the tunnels
c. the opera house   d. the museum

Inference

7. Which statement would a cataphile probably agree with?
a. More police are needed to keep the tunnels safe.
b. The bones should be removed from the tunnels.
c. Only cataphiles should be allowed to explore the tunnels.
d. People should be able to do whatever they want in the tunnels.

Understanding the Functions of Prepositional Phrases

A **prepositional phrase** consists of a preposition (e.g., *to, on, in, of, with, over,* and *down*) and its object. Such phrases (underlined in the examples below) give important, additional details about nouns and verbs. When a prepositional phrase modifies a noun, it answers questions such as **Which one?** or **What kind?**

Examples: *The passage to the chamber was narrow.* **(Which passage?)** / *He is a new type of tourist.* **(Type of what? / What kind?)**

When a prepositional phrase modifies a verb, it answers questions such as **Where?**, **How?**, or **When?**

Examples: *She climbed up the ladder.* **(Where?)** / *Our guide spoke in a loud voice.* **(How?)** / *In May, I visited Paris.* **(When?)**

A. Analyzing. Underline the prepositional phrases in the paragraph below.

I'm standing on a sidewalk in the early morning. The great avenues of Paris are silent, and the shops are closed. From a bakery comes the smell of fresh bread. Suddenly, a man with long hair and a lamp on his head appears from a hole in the sidewalk. He is soon followed by a young woman holding a lantern. Mud covers their boots. The man places the iron cover over the hole and takes the woman's hand. Together, they run down the street, smiling.

B. Completion. Answer the questions below with prepositional phrases from **A**.

1. Where is the writer standing? _____
2. When is this happening? _____
3. Where is the lamp? _____
4. Where does the man put the cover? _____
5. Where does the couple run? _____

Critical Thinking Discuss with a partner. What could be some reasons why visiting Paris's underground is not permitted? Do you think people should be allowed to explore there?

Vocabulary Practice

A. Completion. Complete the information by circling the correct word in each pair.

Much of the network of **1. (sculptures / tunnels)** under Paris is off limits to tourists, with trails that only the cataphiles—and the police—know. However, there is a small section where tourism is allowed. A visitor-friendly legal **2. (entrance / trend)** can be found off Place Denfert-Rochereau, near the Montparnasse district.

∧ Tourists walk through a section of the Paris catacombs that is open to the public.

Here, visitors can walk along skull-and-bone-lined pathways. Tourists are **3. (occupied / permitted)** to take photos in these catacombs. However, most are respectful and **4. (silent / daring)** as they **5. (occupy / descend)** into the catacombs, the final resting place of perhaps six million people. It's a fascinating but strangely sad visit for many people.

B. Words in Context. Complete each sentence with the correct answer.

1. Things that are usually made out of **iron** include _____.

   a. tools   b. shoes

2. A **sculpture** is a work of art made by _____.

   a. painting or drawing   b. shaping stone, wood, or clay

3. If something is described as a **trend**, it is probably becoming _____.

   a. more popular   b. less popular

4. To **descend** a mountain means to _____ it.

   a. go up   b. go down

5. If you **dare** to do something, you are _____ to do it.

   a. brave enough   b. smart enough

> **Word Partnership**
> Use **trend** with: (*v.*) **start a** trend, **follow a** trend;
> (*n.*) **fashion** trend, trend**setter**, **industry** trend; (*adj.*)
> **latest** trend, **current** trend, **downward** trend.

NEW YORK'S UNDERSIDE

Before You Read

A. Definitions. Look at the photo above and read the caption. Match the words in **bold** to their definitions.

1. _____: substances that blow up, breaking things apart suddenly and with great force

2. _____: waste and used water from homes and buildings

3. _____: round holes in a city street used by workers

B. Predict. Look at the headings, photo, and caption on pages 76–77. Check (✓) the information you think you will read about. Then read the passage to check your ideas.

☐ what lies beneath the streets of New York City

☐ what makes working under New York City dangerous

☐ what makes the streets of New York City dangerous

⌃ Each of the 465,000 round steel **manholes** on the streets of New York City is a doorway to an underground network of tunnels. Some—for telephone, TV, or electricity cables—lie just below the surface. Others, carved deep into the earth using **explosives** and huge machines, are for the city's subways, water pipes, and **sewage** system.

A Dangerous Job

1

Since I was a boy, I have always looked down open manholes with curiosity, so I welcomed the **opportunity** to explore and write about the world beneath New York City. With a group of 11

5 "sandhogs"—the nickname[1] for the workers who build New York's underground—I **boarded** a slow, shaky elevator lit by a single light bulb. Slowly we went down a shaft[2] dug through 200 meters of rock. The sandhogs were building a new tunnel to bring water into the city. The present tunnel system carries more than 5.6 billion

10 liters of water every day. That's enough water to fill more than 2,200 Olympic-sized swimming pools.

As we descended, it got dark and the air got cool. I looked up into darkness and down into deeper blackness, then the elevator stopped, and everyone got out. Then came the hard part, climbing

15 another 10 meters down a long, **slippery** metal ladder.[3] At the bottom was a dark tunnel filled with dust and smoke. Sandhogs were using explosives like dynamite[4] to cut through the solid rock. The tunnel extends slowly—only four meters a day—and with each day come new dangers. Sandhogs live in constant fear of being

20 hurt by sharp pieces of exploded rock. Their bodies are covered in such scars.[5]

"Why do this work?" I asked Brian Gallagher, a sandhog for 16 years. Brian's father was a sandhog, too, but it is not tradition that brought him here. "It's the money," he said. An **experienced**

25 sandhog earns over $100,000 a year. The rewards are well deserved. A sandhog's chances of dying on the job are far greater than those of an above-ground construction worker, or even a New York City police officer. "Everything down here can kill you," one sandhog said. They know many more workers will die before

30 the tunnel is completed.

A River of Sewage

On another trip below the city, sewer worker Jeff Kwami showed me how the city's sewage is kept **flowing** smoothly. We went down a manhole wearing plastic bodysuits, gloves, and tanks of air.

35 Everything around us was wet and slippery, as we climbed carefully down 12 meters and then stopped on a narrow **concrete** step. In

∧ "Sandhogs" at work deep under New York City

---

1 A **nickname** is an informal and unofficial name.

2 A **shaft** is a vertical tunnel.

3 A **ladder** is a structure made for climbing on.

4 **Dynamite** is an explosive substance.

5 A **scar** is a mark left on the skin after a wound or an injury has healed.

front of me was a fast-moving river of sewage nearly two meters wide. It smelled **awful**. I asked Kwami, "What happens if you fall in and you're not attached to a rope?" He said if you didn't pull yourself out, you'd **drown** in the sewage. But unlike the dangers sandhogs face, such situations are rare. As we move through the sewer, Kwami seems calm and **confident**, but it's still a terrifying thought.

Later, as we left the darkness and danger below, Kwami **joked**, "See any alligators?" Over the years, there have been stories about giant alligators living in the sewers. I tell Kwami that in 1935, the *New York Times* reported an alligator was pulled from a sewer. He still didn't believe it, and we laugh together as we climb back to the surface.

— **Adapted from** *Under New York* **by Joel Swerdlow, National Geographic Magazine**

Reading Comprehension

Multiple Choice. Choose the best answer for each question.

Inference
1. The writer of the passage is _____.
   a. considering getting a job as a tunnel worker
   b. taking tourists into New York City's tunnels
   c. interested in what lies beneath New York City
   d. reporting on the benefits of working underground

Detail
2. What danger that underground workers face is NOT mentioned?
   a. slipping   b. being cut by rock
   c. drowning   d. elevators falling

Detail
3. Why does Brian Gallagher work as a sandhog?
   a. He enjoys danger.   b. It's a family tradition.
   c. The job pays well. d. The work is easy to do.

Inference
4. Sewer workers probably carry tanks of air because _____.
   a. the smell of the sewage is bad
   b. the tunnel is filled with smoke
   c. they have to dive into the sewage
   d. they need to clean the air in the sewer

Detail
5. Which of these is the most dangerous job mentioned?
   a. sandhog   b. police officer
   c. sewer worker   d. construction worker

Detail
6. Which of these things about being a sewer worker is NOT mentioned?
   a. It's useful to wear a bodysuit.
   b. It's easy to get wet.
   c. The pay is very high.
   d. A rope could save your life.

Main Idea
7. What would be the best heading for the last paragraph?
   a. Recent Alligator Sighting
   b. The 80-Year-Old Alligator
   c. How to Survive Sewage
   d. Just a Story?

Did You Know?

Stories such as "the alligator in the sewer" are known as urban legends—modern stories of unknown origin that are often believed to be true, but are usually not.

Breaking Down Long Sentences

Long sentences can be easier to analyze and understand if you break them into shorter parts called *clauses*.

1. To identify a clause, first circle each key verb in the text.

2. Find the subject and object (or complement) of each verb. Underline the subject and double-underline the object.

3. Draw parentheses around modifiers (such as adjectives, prepositional phrases, and adverbs).

4. Look at each set of verb, subject, and object (or complement). Look at the words around them. This is a clause. Each clause has its own idea. Divide the sentence into its main clauses. Draw slash marks to separate them.

The first sentence of the reading on pages 76–77 can be broken down like this:

Since I (was) a boy, /I have (always) (looked) down open manholes (with curiosity), /so I (welcomed) the opportunity (to explore and write about the world beneath New York City.)

A. Analyzing. Read this sentence from the passage. Use the tips above to break it into smaller parts.

I looked up into darkness and down into deeper blackness, then the elevator stopped, and everyone got out.

B. Analyzing. Now use the tips to break down the text below from the passage.

With a group of 11 "sandhogs"—the nickname for the workers who build New York's underground—I boarded a slow, shaky elevator lit by a single light bulb. Slowly we went down a shaft dug through 200 meters of rock.

Critical Thinking Discuss with a partner. Why are jobs like tunnel workers (sandhogs) and sewer workers particularly dangerous? What do you think are the most dangerous jobs? Why do people do them?

∧ Some tunnels under New York City are over 200 meters deep, and building them can be dangerous.

Vocabulary Practice

A. Completion. Complete the information with words from the box.
One word is extra.

awful   board   concrete   experienced   flowed   joked   opportunity

Under the **1.** _____ buildings of New York City lies one of
its greatest attractions—its subway system. It runs 24 hours a day,
365 days a year. On a typical weekday, over five million people
2. _____ a train at one of hundreds of stations. More
3. _____ travelers can manage the system easily, but
first-time visitors can find it confusing.

Nevertheless, if you get a(n) **4.** _____, a ride on the subway
is an experience worth having and can sometimes provide really
interesting sights. For example, in August 2013, a dead shark was
found in a subway car. No one knows who put it there, or why. But
since the subway is often quite dirty, some people **5.** _____
that the **6.** _____ smell was not that unusual!

B. Completion. Complete the sentences using the words in the box.
One word is extra.

confident   drowned   flowed   joke   slippery

1. Many of the steps leading down to New York's subway can be
   _____ when wet.

2. For someone new to the New York subway system, the crowds can be
   scary. The secret is to be _____ and keep moving.

3. In 2012, Hurricane Sandy caused serious flooding to the New York
   subway when water from the storm _____ into the subway stations
   and tunnels.

4. It's been estimated that there are as many rats in New York's subway as
   there are people. Thousands of these rats _____ in the floods
   caused by the 2012 storm.

> ∨ A rat

> **Thesaurus awful** Also look up: (*adj.*) *terrible,*
> *horrible, dreadful*

VIEWING Sewer Diver

Before You Watch

A. Preview. Look at the photo and read the caption. Then discuss the questions below with a partner.

Sewer divers like Carlos Barrios and Julio Cou Cámara (pictured here) have a dirty and dangerous job.

1. What exactly do you think Carlos Barrios and Julio Cou Cámara do in their job?
2. Do you think they enjoy their work?

B. Predict. Which of these things do you think you can find in the sewers?

☐ human waste   ☐ bodies   ☐ dirty water
☐ chairs   ☐ garbage   ☐ bones
☐ cars   ☐ clean water   ☐ dead animals

While You Watch

A. Viewing. As you watch, check (✓) the things above that the video mentions. Were your ideas correct?

B. Categorizing. Which of the things in **A** does Carlos Barrios take out of the sewer?

After You Watch

A. Multiple Choice. Choose the best answer to each question.

1. Which city does Carlos Barrios work in?

   a. Los Angeles   b. New York City   c. Mexico City

2. What does Carlos Barrios do in the sewers?

   a. He cleans the sewer walls.

   b. He tests the safety of the water.

   c. He removes objects that block the sewers.

3. What advice does Julio give Carlos Barrios before a job?

   a. Be calm and careful.

   b. Don't touch anything sharp.

   c. Wear a good dive suit.

4. What is Carlos Barrios afraid of while in the sewer?

   a. getting a cut   b. getting lost   c. drowning

5. After diving, what does Carlos Barrios need to do?

   a. get washed and cleaned

   b. put on a different suit

   c. stop by the hospital

B. Discuss. Discuss these questions with a partner.

1. What do you think are the biggest challenges Carlos Barrios faces?

2. Do you think you could do Carlos Barrios' job? Why or why not?

3. What other dirty or dangerous jobs can you name?

❮ Carlos Barrios is lowered into a river of sewage.

6

REEF ENCOUNTERS

In a reef off the Izu Peninsula in Japan, a moray eel swims among the branches of soft coral.

Warm Up

Discuss these questions with a partner.

1. What do you like most about the ocean?

2. Which ocean animals do you think are dangerous?

3. Do you think humans have damaged parts of the world's oceans? How?

Before You Read

A. True or False. Look at the picture and read the caption. Which of the statements about coral reefs (1–4) below are true (**T**), and which are false (**F**)?

1. Coral reefs are usually found in warm water.   **T**   **F**
2. Coral polyps are a type of plant.   **T**   **F**
3. A coral reef usually gets smaller over time.   **T**   **F**
4. Some coral reefs are very old.   **T**   **F**

B. Predict. Look quickly at the title, headings, photos, and captions on pages 84–87. Check (☒) the information you think you will read about. Then read the passage to check your ideas.

☐ How coral reefs are formed
☐ Coral reef wildlife
☐ Problems affecting reefs
☐ Threats to coral fishermen

∧ Mostly found in water warmed by sunlight, reefs like this one are built by coral polyps.[1] Over time, as more and more coral polyps come together, the reef grows. Some of the coral reefs on the planet today began growing over 50 million years ago.

---

1 **Polyps** are tiny, soft-bodied animals related to jellyfish.

Cities Beneath the Sea

1 For uncounted **generations**, trillions[1] upon trillions of tiny creatures called coral polyps have lived and died, leaving behind a substance called limestone. A building material prized throughout the history of mankind, limestone was used to
5 construct the Great Pyramids of Egypt, as well as **countless** churches and castles. Even today, crushed limestone is used to make the cement[2] with which modern structures are built. For this, coral polyps are sometimes called "the animals that helped make the world." Yet, the greatest limestone structures in the
10 world are built underwater, by the coral polyps themselves. We call them reefs. They are larger in scale than buildings made by any other living beings, including humans.

A Variety of Life

Indeed, a living coral reef is **remarkable**, a "city beneath
15 the sea," filled with a rich variety of life. Coral reefs **thrive** in warm, **shallow** oceans near the equator, and are among the world's most colorful places. Each reef is full of **brilliantly** colored fish and coral forming wonderful patterns. In addition

1 A **trillion** is 1,000,000,000,000.
2 **Cement** is a gray powder that is mixed with sand and water to make a hard, solid substance.

to their beauty, the reefs are an important food source for
20 fish, and for humans. In fact, reef fish make up a significant
percentage of the global fish catch.

Threats to Coral Reefs

Various human activities can cause great harm to the world's
coral reefs. For example, reefs can be damaged when the
25 coral is taken for use in building materials, jewelry-making,
or to fill aquariums.[3]

Illegal fishing methods like blast and cyanide fishing also
harm the reefs. These methods can help fishermen get a
good catch, but their **negative** effects on the reefs are
30 significant. Blast fishing involves setting off bombs in the
water to kill as many fish as possible. The blasts kill most
living things nearby and cause damage to the reef's structure.

In cyanide fishing, fishermen release liquid cyanide, a very
dangerous and deadly chemical, into the reef. As a result, the
35 fish become stunned.[4] This makes them easy to collect. The
fishermen can then sell them for big money to the aquarium
market, or for **consumption** in restaurants. Meanwhile, the
reef is damaged by the cyanide which kills large numbers of
coral polyps, and by the fishermen who break apart the reef
40 looking for the stunned fish.

Another threat to a reef is water **pollution**. When floods[5] in
Australia covered the Great Barrier Reef with dirty freshwater,
the quality of the water changed, and chemicals killed the
reef life. This is happening to many reefs around the world.
45 In addition, due to global warming, many reefs have become
sick, turning white in a process known as coral bleaching.

Reasons for Hope

These threats to coral reefs are very serious, but there is
reason to hope that they will survive. If we take steps toward
50 coral reef **conservation**, it is likely that these tiny creatures,
which survived natural threats for millions of years, will be
able to rebuild the reefs that so much ocean life depends on.

---

3 An **aquarium** is a tank or building where sea animals are kept.

4 If an animal is **stunned**, it is confused or hurt and unable to move.

5 A **flood** is a large amount of water covering an area of land that is usually dry.

Spot-banded butterflyfish

Residents of the Reef

Coral reefs occupy less than one percent of the
surface area of the world's oceans, but they
provide a home for 25 percent of
all marine fish species. Here
are some examples of the
creatures that call a
coral reef home.

Blue-girdled angelfish

Redfin butterflyfish

∧ A long-snouted seahorse
"stands" between coral branches.

∧ A nudibranch uses its vivid colors
to tell predators to stay away.

∧ Jellyfish are not actually fish. They
have no brain, blood, or bones.

Reading Comprehension

Multiple Choice. Choose the best answer for each question.

Gist

1. What is this passage mainly about?
   a. the underwater world in general
   b. the use of coral in the building of cities
   c. the kinds of animals found near coral reefs
   d. the beauty of reefs and the dangers they face

Detail

2. The material commonly called coral is made of _____.
   a. shells   b. reefs
   c. polyps   d. cement

Detail

3. Which statement about coral reefs is NOT true?
   a. They are an important source of fish.
   b. They are usually found in deep ocean waters.
   c. They are among the world's most colorful places.
   d. They can be larger than structures made by humans.

Vocabulary

4. The word *scale* in line 11 is closest in meaning to _____.
   a. weight   b. number of fish
   c. size   d. length of time

Detail

5. Why do some fishermen use the method of blast fishing?
   a. to catch fish for aquariums
   b. to kill as many fish as possible
   c. to release liquid cyanide into the reef
   d. to break apart the reef to find stunned fish

Did You Know?

Doctors sometimes use coral to replace missing pieces of bone in their patients.

Inference

6. Why does the author mention that the fishermen sell reef fish for *big money* (line 36)?
   a. to give a reason reefs should be saved
   b. to excuse the fishermen who use illegal methods
   c. to compare the effects of blast and cyanide fishing
   d. to show why such illegal fishing methods are attractive

Main Idea

7. Which sentence best expresses the main idea of the final paragraph?
   a. Coral polyps and reefs are in little danger.
   b. It is too late for us to save the coral reefs.
   c. With our help, coral reefs can continue to survive.
   d. Coral reefs are in danger because they are very old and can break easily.

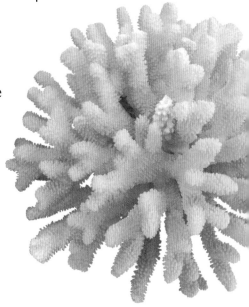

Understanding Cause and Effect Relationships

A *cause* is an action that makes something happen. An *effect* is a result of that action. Certain connecting words are used to show cause and effect relationships. In these examples, the cause is *the heavy rain* and the effect is *the flood*.

The heavy rain **caused / resulted in / was the reason for** *the flood.*

There was heavy rain. **Therefore, / Consequently, / As a result**, *there was a flood.*

There was heavy rain, **so** *there was a flood.*

Because of / As a result of *the heavy rain, there was a flood.*

A. Analyzing. Circle the causes and underline the effects in the text below.

Not all reefs begin naturally. For example, an ocean current may encounter a man-made object, like a sunken ship. As a result, the water around the ship may become rich with tiny animals called plankton. A lot of small fish gather there to feed on the plankton. Consequently, larger animals are attracted to the ship. Because the ship has many little openings, many creatures also have a place to hide. In time, the ship becomes covered in polyps. As a result, soon, it no longer looks like a ship at all.

B. Completion. Use the information in **A** to complete the chart below.

Causes	Effects
1. ocean current encounters sunken ship	
2. a lot of small fish gather there to feed	
3.	many creatures have a place to hide
4.	

Critical Thinking Discuss with a partner. What do you think should be done to save the coral reefs? Who do you think should do it?

Vocabulary Practice

A. Definitions. Read the information below. Then match each word in **red** with its definition.

> Not all coral is found in warm, **shallow** water. Some coral polyps can survive, even **thrive**, in the cold water at the bottom of the ocean. But even there, they're not safe from threats. Fishing boats—called bottom trawlers—pull heavy nets across the ocean floor. The nets have a very **negative** effect on deep sea coral and the **remarkable** sea life around them. Because the **conservation** of these corals is important for future **generations** of sea life, the U.S. has a law that prevents bottom-trawling in over a million square kilometers of ocean off its Pacific coast.

1. harmful or bad _____
2. the opposite of *deep* _____
3. special and amazing _____
4. live and grow successfully _____
5. taking care of the environment _____
6. groups of living things of a similar age _____

∧ In bottom-trawling, heavy nets are held open by metal "trawl doors." Each door weighs over 5,500 kilograms, and damages sea life as it is dragged across the sea floor.

B. Words in Context. Complete each sentence with the correct answer.

1. You and your parents are members of _____ **generation(s)**.

   a. the same   b. different

2. If you **consume** a fish, you _____ it.

   a. eat   b. cook

3. An example of something **countless** would be _____.

   a. balloons at a party   b. the sand on a beach

4. If water is **polluted**, it is probably _____ to drink.

   a. safe   b. unsafe

5. A color that is described as **brilliant** is probably _____.

   a. bright and vivid   b. very dark

> **Word Partnership**
> Use *negative* with:
> (*n.*) negative **effect**, negative **experience**, negative **image**, negative **attitude**, negative **thoughts**, negative **comment**, negative **response**.

The Truth about Great Whites

Before You Read

> Great white sharks are actually mostly gray. The word *white* refers to the shark's bottom-side.

A. Completion. Complete the information with the words from the box.

fish	length	nets	teeth	whales

Great White Shark Facts

Type: Like all sharks, great whites are a type of **1.** _____.

Size: They are 4.6 to 6 meters in **2.** _____. (They can be longer than a bus!)

Weight: They can weigh up to 3,000 kilograms or more.

Jaws: They have up to 300 **3.** _____ in several rows.

Food: Their diet includes fish, seals, sea lions, and small **4.** _____.

Threats: They are threatened by overfishing and accidental catching in **5.** _____.

Situation: Endangered.

B. Predict. What do you think is meant by the title "The Truth About Great Whites"? Discuss with a partner. Then, read the passage on pages 92–93 to check your ideas.

Shark Attack

In sunny California, Craig Rogers was sitting on his surfboard,[1] scanning the distance for his next wave, when his board suddenly stopped moving. He looked down and was terrified to see a great white shark **biting** the front of his board. "I could have touched its eye with my elbow," says Craig. The shark had surfaced so quietly, he didn't hear a thing. In his **horror** and **confusion**, he waved his arms and accidentally cut two of his fingers on the shark's teeth. He got off the opposite side of his surfboard, into the water. Then, with Craig in the water, blood flowing from his fingers, the five-meter-long shark simply swam away.

Over a hundred shark attacks happen each year. Of these, one third are said to be great white attacks. As a result, great whites are often **categorized** as "man-eaters" and thought to hunt and kill humans. However, this is factually **inaccurate**, since great whites rarely kill their human **victims**. In fact, a person has a greater chance of being killed by lightning[2] than by a great white. With frightening jaws that hold around 300 teeth **arranged** in several rows, a great white could very easily kill a person. Yet, surprisingly, most great white victims live to tell the tale. Shark researchers are trying to comprehend the reasons great whites attack people, and why most of those people manage to escape a horrible death.

---

1 A **surfboard** is a long, narrow board used for surfing.
2 **Lightning** is the bright flashes of light and electricity in the sky that happen during rainstorms.

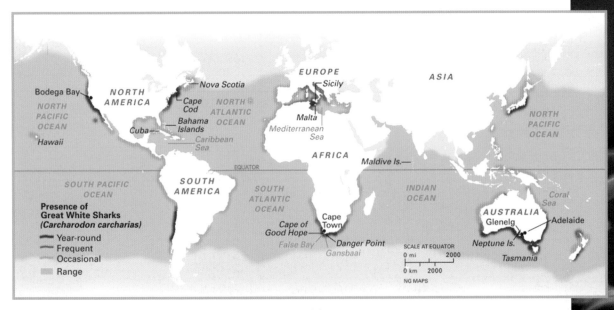

⌃ Great whites can be found in seas all over the world. In some places, like off Australia and the southern coast of Africa, they are protected.

One of the most common explanations for great white attacks is that great whites don't see well. It is thought that they often mistake a person for a seal or a sea lion—a very **tempting** snack to a great white. But there

25 is reason to doubt this. Some research now shows that great whites can actually see, and identify seals, very well. When attacking seals, great whites shoot up to the surface and bite with great force. However, when they approach humans, they often move in slowly and bite less hard. "They take a bite, feel them over, then move on," says Peter Klimley,

30 author of *The Secret Lives of Sharks*.

Shark experts like Klimley **hypothesize** that great whites "attack" because they are actually curious animals that like to investigate things. They believe that it's possible that great whites use their bite not just to kill and eat, but also to **gather** information. According to this idea, once a

35 great white identifies what it is biting, it simply lets go.

Even though such experiences are unlucky for people like Craig Rogers, perhaps when sharks bite surfboards, other objects, or even people, they are likely just trying to learn what they are.

A great white glides through the water. Great whites can swim at speeds of up to 40 kilometers an hour

Multiple Choice. Choose the best answer for each question.

Gist

1. Another title for this passage could be _____.
   a. Surfers and Sharks: Unlikely Friends
   b. How to Survive a Shark Attack
   c. Why Great Whites Kill Humans
   d. Great Whites: Facts and Fiction

Detail

2. After Craig Rogers fell into the water, _____.
   a. the shark swam away
   b. the shark attacked him
   c. the shark bit his fingers
   d. the shark bit his surfboard

Detail

3. According to the author, it is difficult to understand why great whites _____.
   a. kill humans
   b. have so many teeth
   c. often let humans escape
   d. grow to six meters or more

Purpose

4. What is the purpose of the third paragraph?
   a. to explain why great whites don't see well
   b. to describe how great whites hunt for seals
   c. to provide advice on what to do if you see a great white
   d. to give possible reasons why great whites don't kill humans

Vocabulary

5. Which of the following words is closest in meaning to *doubt* in line 25?
   a. not believe   b. be curious about
   c. be afraid of   d. think deeply about

Reference

6. In line 29, the word *them* refers to _____.
   a. people   b. teeth
   c. great whites   d. seals

Fact or Theory?

7. Which statement is a fact and not a theory?
   a. Great whites are curious animals.
   b. Great whites are not able to see well.
   c. Great whites bite to get information.
   d. Great whites eat seals and sea lions.

Did You Know?

A great white shark tooth (pictured here in actual size) can measure more than 6 centimeters (2.5 inches) long.

Recognizing Contrastive Relationships

Some connecting words can be used to show contrast. Notice their placement and punctuation in the following examples.

I'm an excellent swimmer, **but** / **yet** *I rarely go swimming.*

I'm an excellent swimmer. **However,** *I rarely go swimming.*

Though / **Although** / **Even though** *I'm afraid of the water, I went swimming.*

I went swimming **though** / **although** / **even though** *I'm afraid of the water.*

Despite / **In spite of** *the bad weather, I went swimming in the sea.*

I went swimming in the sea **despite** / **in spite of** *the bad weather.*

A. Joining Sentences. Using the words in parentheses, rewrite each set of sentences below to form a single sentence.

1. Sharks are dangerous animals. Many people also think they're beautiful.

   _____ (yet)

2. Seals and sea lions may look similar. They are actually very different species.

   _____ (although)

3. Many people think great whites are the biggest fish on Earth. Whale sharks are much bigger.

   _____ (but)

4. There are many shark warning signs on that beach. People still go swimming there.

   _____ (despite)

⌄ From below, surfers on their boards can sometimes look "seal-shaped." Some scientists believe this is why sharks attack them.

Critical Thinking Discuss with a partner. What theories does the author provide for why great whites attack people? Which theory do you think is the most believable? Can you think of any other reasons?

A. Completion. Choose the correct words to complete the sentences.

1. When they are out at sea, shark researchers put food in the water. The (**tempting** / **confusing**) smell of the food makes the sharks come close enough for the scientists to study them.

2. Whale sharks, the largest sharks in the world, never bite or chew, although they have thousands of tiny teeth (**categorized** / **arranged**) in more than 300 rows.

3. Scientists (**arrange** / **hypothesize**) that the decline in the number of sharks may be related to overfishing.

4. Each year, great white sharks (**gather** / **tempt**) near Cape Town to eat seals, which are plentiful in South Africa's water.

5. The International Union for the Conservation of Nature (**gathers** / **categorizes**) hundreds of shark species as endangered.

B. Completion. Complete the information with words from the box. One word is extra.

arrange	bite	confusion	horror	inaccurate	victims

In 1974, writer Peter Benchley wrote the famous novel *Jaws*, about a killer shark that hunts its human **1.** _____. The next year, Steven Spielberg made a movie of the same name. While the movie was exciting, it led to some **2.** _____ about the true nature of great whites. The movie made the great white into a symbol of **3.** _____ and death. However, the behavior of the shark shown in *Jaws* is actually quite **4.** _____. The truth is that great whites rarely **5.** _____ humans. Years later, Benchley and Spielberg both felt bad about spreading false information about these creatures. In his later life, Benchley worked to educate people with more factual information about great white sharks.

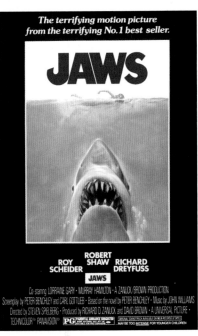

A poster for the movie *Jaws*, which is famous for its scary "shark" music, made up of only two notes

> **Word Link**
> *in–* can be added to some words to form the opposite meaning, e.g., *inaccurate*, *inability*, *inaction*.

VIEWING Swimming with Sharks

Before You Watch

∧ In Baja, Mexico, divers take photographs of a great white shark from the safety of a cage.

A. Definitions. Here are some words and phrases you will hear in the video. Match the words and phrases to their definitions.

1. ban • • a. silly, not wise
2. foolish • • b. to disallow something
3. investigate • • c. to come so close to something you touch it
4. associate with • • d. to link or connect in the mind or imagination
5. brush up against • • e. to examine something in order to discover the truth

B. Predict. Look at the picture above and read the caption. Then read the statements (1–3) below. Do you think they are true (**T**) or false (**F**)? As you watch the video, check your answers.

1. In the video, there are children swimming with sharks.   T   F
2. Sharks bite more people than dogs do.   T   F
3. In Florida, people are allowed to swim with sharks.   T   F

While You Watch

A. Completion. Read the sentences (1–5) below. As you watch the video, circle the correct answers to complete each sentence.

1. In 2002, (**Hawaii / Florida / California**) became the first U.S. state to ban the feeding of marine wildlife.

2. Bull, reef, and lemon sharks (**often / occasionally / never**) attack divers.

3. Bob Dimond wants to (**control / ban / increase**) the feeding of sharks.

4. Shark feeding has (**often / rarely / never**) been directly associated with attacks on humans.

5. When a shark strikes a human, it is described as a (**"hit and run" / "rip and release" / "bump and bite"**).

After You Watch

A. Matching. Using information from the video, match the causes with the effects.

Causes	Effects
1. more people are going shark diving •	• a. there was a lot of negative publicity
2. there were many shark attacks one summer •	• b. national parks ban the feeding of animals
3. sharks associate humans with food •	• c. there will be increased chances that they will attack humans
4. feeding wild animals makes them more likely to attack humans •	• d. questions are raised about how close people should get to sharks

B. Discussion. Discuss these questions with a partner.

1. Would you pay to swim with sharks? Why or why not?

2. Do you think swimming with sharks should be banned?

3. Bob Dimond thinks that all shark feeding should be banned. Do you agree? Why or why not?

To get sharks to come close, shark tours often put food in the water. Sharks can smell this food from far away. >

7

SWEET SCENTS

A closeup of a water lily. The aroma of some flowers contains up to 100 different chemicals, and is used to tempt insects to come near them.

Warm Up

Discuss these questions with a partner.

1. How many kinds of flowers can you name in English? Make a list.

2. Which flower do you think is the most beautiful? Which do you think has the best scent?

3. What are some of the ways in which people use flowers?

Before You Read

A. Definitions. Match the words below (1–4) to their definitions.

1. cut flowers •   • a. a container to hold flowers

2. fragrance •   • b. a nice smell

3. vase •   • c. a person or a store that sells flowers

4. florist •   • d. flowers that are taken off the plant

B. Scan. Read the title, look at the pictures, and read the first and last sentences of each paragraph. Scan the reading for anything else that stands out. What is the reading about?

a. the condition of cut flowers around the world

b. the international business of cut flowers

c. technology in the cut flower business

THE FLOWER TRADE

Aalsmeer, Netherlands

1　When you purchase fresh-cut flowers, do you think about where they came from? It might **make sense** to think they were grown somewhere nearby. The reality, though, is that the cut flower trade is increasingly international. Today,
5　thanks to airplanes and high-tech cooling systems, even the most delicate[1] flower can be **exported**, and sold in a florist thousands of kilometers away from where it was grown.

The Cut Flower Leader

The country that **dominates** the world cut flower trade is
10　the Netherlands. It **handles** about 60 percent of the world's cut flowers. And its auction houses[2] are very large indeed— Aalsmeer, near Amsterdam, is an auction house in the sense that Tokyo is a city, or Everest a mountain. About 120 soccer fields would fill its main building. Nineteen million flowers
15　are sold here on an average day, including roses, lilies, and of course, tulips.

The heart of the global flower trade, Aalsmeer processes 19 million flowers every day.

1 Something **delicate** is easy to damage and needs to be treated carefully.

2 **Auction houses** are companies that hold public sales where the price of an item is not yet decided and customers compete to buy it.

The Netherlands is also a world leader in developing new flower varieties. Dutch companies and the government **invest** a **considerable** amount of money in flower research. Their scientists
20 look for ways to lengthen a flower's vase life,[3] to strengthen flowers to **prevent** them from being damaged while traveling, and also to strengthen the natural fragrance of the flowers.

At Aalsmeer, delicate orchid plants are prepared for auction.

The Benefits of Climate

Despite the Netherlands' dominance of the flower market, there
25 are many places with a better climate for growing flowers, and the climate of Ecuador is almost perfect. Mauricio Dávalos is the man responsible for starting Ecuador's flower industry. "Our biggest edge is nature," he **claims**. "Our roses are the best in the world." With **predictable** rainy periods and 12 hours of sunlight
30 each day, Ecuador's roses are **renowned** for their large heads and long, straight stems. Every year, Ecuador sells about 500 million flowers to the U.S. alone. The industry has brought employment opportunities and a stronger economy to regions of the country. "My family has TV now. There are radios," says Yolanda Quishpe,
35 20, who picked roses for four years.

To others, the increasingly international nature of the flower trade is very bad news. In recent years, local growers in the U.S. faced huge competition from international flower companies, and many lost their businesses. Lina Hale, an independent rose grower in
40 California, said her father had predicted the situation in the 1980s. "I see a freight train coming down the track," he warned her, "and it's coming straight towards us."

---

3 **Vase life** means the amount of time a cut flower remains in good condition.

From Colombia to the U.S.

How a rose travels from mountain to vase in just three days.

Tuesday, 7 A.M.

Roses are cut in the cool mountain air of Colombia and moved quickly to indoor cooling houses.

Tuesday, 1 P.M.

Workers categorize the roses based on size, stem length, shape, and color.

Wednesday, 6 A.M.

Roses are boxed and sent to Bogotá Airport for the 3.5-hour flight to Miami.

Wednesday, 8 P.M.

Roses are checked by officials, and then transported by truck, train, or plane.

Thursday, 4 P.M.

Roses arrive at large markets in major U.S. cities, where they are purchased by flower sellers.

Beautiful Bqt. $12 99 a bunch

Reading Comprehension

Multiple Choice. Choose the best answer for each question.

Main Idea

1. What is the main idea of the first paragraph?
   a. Cut flowers can't survive a long trip.
   b. You should buy flowers from local florists.
   c. Flowers you buy come from faraway places.
   d. It's important to think about where you buy your flowers.

Detail

2. Which statement about Aalsmeer's auction house is true?
   a. It's very large.
   b. It's as big as Tokyo.
   c. It handles 60% of the Netherlands' exports.
   d. Nineteen million flowers are grown there.

Detail

3. Which of the following are mentioned as large investors in flower research?
   a. American companies and their government
   b. private companies and the Dutch government
   c. Ecuador's local flower growers and pickers
   d. airplane and high-tech cooling companies

Vocabulary

4. The word *edge* in line 28 is closest in meaning to _____.
   a. end   b. advantage
   c. angle   d. difference

Detail

5. The author uses Yolanda Quishpe's quote in line 34 to ____.
   a. show that flowers from Ecuador are beautiful
   b. show that the flower trade in Ecuador helps the locals
   c. show that Ecuador could grow even more flowers
   d. show that rose-picking is a very popular job in Ecuador

Inference

6. What did Lina Hale's father mean when he said, *I see a freight train coming down the track* (line 41)?
   a. He could actually see a train.
   b. He knew his business would be threatened.
   c. He thought customers wouldn't want roses.
   d. He thought trains were the new way to move flowers.

Purpose

7. The purpose of the "From Colombia to the U.S." section is to _____.
   a. show how the international cut flower trade works
   b. list reasons why Colombian roses are expensive
   c. illustrate why roses have much longer vase lives
   d. explain why Colombian roses always look fresh

Did You Know?

The number one importer of cut flowers in the world is Germany. Germans have a special passion for roses, most of which they buy from the Dutch.

Reading Skill

Determining Similarities and Differences

When a text contains detailed information on two or more topics, it can be helpful to consider how they are similar or different. One way to present similarities and differences visually is with overlapping circles. This is called a Venn diagram. Here is how we might classify details of roses and orchids using a Venn diagram.

Roses
- 15,000 species
- easy to grow

Both
- grown for export
- bright colors

Orchids
- 25,000 species
- difficult to grow

A. Completion. What else do you know about roses and orchids? Add the characteristics (a–c) to the Venn diagram above.

a. nice fragrance   b. most popular in red   c. popular house plant

B. Classification. Look back at the reading on pages 101–103. Match each characteristic (a–f) with the country or countries it describes to complete the Venn diagram.

a. grows roses
b. holds huge flower auctions
c. has 12 hours of sunlight a day
d. dominates the flower export trade
e. has an ideal climate for growing flowers
f. benefits economically from the flower trade

Netherlands   **Both**   **Ecuador**

Critical Thinking Discuss with a partner. Why do you think there is such a strong international demand for flowers? Do you think the flower trade is a good business to be involved in? Why or why not?

Vocabulary Practice

A. Completion. Complete the information below using the words and phrases from the box. One word is extra.

considerable	exported	handle	makes sense	prevents

Tuesday, 7 A.M.   Workers cut the roses in the early morning.
It **1.** _____ to do this as early as possible,
because the air then is cool. The cool air
2. _____ the roses from drying out. The
workers then sort and prepare the roses for travel.

Wednesday, 6 A.M.   The roses are put in boxes and trucked to Bogotá
Airport to be **3.** _____ to the U.S.

Thursday, 4 P.M.   The roses arrive at markets in various U.S. cities. These
markets **4.** _____ the huge task of sorting the
flowers. Then the flowers are sent to the city's florists.

B. Words in Context. Complete each sentence with the correct answer.

1. A company that **dominates** other companies _____.
   a. beats them in business   b. assists them

2. If someone pays a **considerable** amount, they pay a fairly _____ amount.
   a. high   b. low

3. Something that is **claimed** to be true is _____ true.
   a. definitely   b. said to be

4. If a country is **renowned** for its flowers, it is _____ for them.
   a. disliked   b. well known

5. Someone who is **predictable** behaves _____ each time you meet.
   a. the same way   b. very differently

6. When you **invest** in something, you _____.
   a. put effort or money into it   b. get money or things from it

> **Word Partnership**
> Use **handle** with:
> (*n.*) handle **a job/a
> problem/a situation**;
> handle **pressure/
> responsibility**; (*adj.*)
> **difficult/easy/hard
> to** handle.

THE POWER OF
PERFUME

To sell perfumes, companies often try to connect their products with ideas of wealth, style, or well-being. Even the shape of the bottle is carefully considered in hopes of attracting customers to the brand.

Before You Read

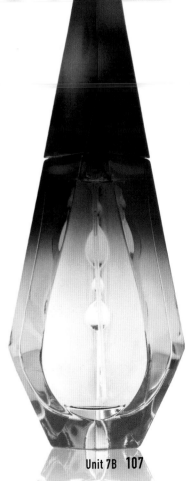

A. Discuss. Look at the pictures and read the caption. Then answer the questions below.

1. Which bottle do you think is the most attractive? What do you like about it?

2. Which of these bottles do you think contains a fragrance for a man, for a woman, or for both?

B. Scan. Why does the passage on pages 108–109 mention baseball player Derek Jeter? Scan the reading to find out. Then share your answers with a partner.

A Promise in a Bottle

"Perfume," says expert perfumer Sophia Grojsman, "is a promise in a bottle."
That promise might be reflected in a perfume's name: *Joy*[1] or *Pleasure*, for
example. Millions of dollars are spent on the marketing of a perfume so that
5   customers connect luxury, attraction, or a certain attitude to a fragrance.

Fragrances can have power over our thoughts and emotions. Scientists
believe memory and smell are closely connected in our brains, and that
certain aromas have the power to call up deep memories. Perfume makers
are especially aware of this and use aromas that touch us deeply.

10   In the perfume world, an **essence** is a material with its own special aroma.
Some are natural, and **derived** from flowers and plants, for example.
Others are synthetic[2] copies of rare or difficult-to-**obtain** essences. Perfume
authority Harry Frémont says a good fragrance "is a balance between
naturals and synthetics. Naturals give richness and roundness; synthetics,
15   backbone and sparkle."

Hundreds of new perfumes are put on the market every year. Of these, few
become successful. It's a risky business. A company introducing a new scent
can easily run through a **budget** of 20 million dollars. Profits, however, can
be very high. One successful fragrance, *CK One* from designer Calvin Klein,
20   made 250 million dollars in its first year.

Perfume making is both a
science and an art. To make
a good perfume, scientists
(left) must work with scent
experts (right) to find and
mix the right scents.

Image and Marketing

In a Paris perfume store, a building of shining stone, metal, and glass, famous perfumes are **displayed** and **guarded** like the works of art in the nearby Louvre Museum.[3] Salespeople are dressed
25 smartly in black, and each type of perfume is sold in a **distinctively** shaped bottle. In perfume sales, the **emphasis** is on presentation at least as much as on the product.

So, naturally, France's main competitor in the global perfume market is the United States, where image is all-important. Celebrity-branded
30 scents fill the market, each **preceded** by floods of print ads and TV appearances designed to create hype. Even sports celebrities, like baseball star Derek Jeter, are creating their own fragrance brands.

It is easy to be confused about which perfume to buy. Perfumer Annie Buzantian offers this advice: You really can't get an idea
35 whether a perfume works or not until you wear it. "It's like the difference between a dress on the hanger and a dress on your body," says Buzantian. Though Frémont adds, "Your first impression is often the right one."

Baseball player Derek Jeter advertises his scent, a cologne named *Driven*.

---

1 **Joy** is a feeling of happiness.
2 If a material is **synthetic**, it is made by humans.
3 The **Louvre Museum** is a world-famous art museum located in Paris, France.

Reading Comprehension

Multiple Choice. Choose the best answer for each question.

Main Idea

1. What is the main idea of the first paragraph?
   a. The perfume industry uses marketing to sell ideas.
   b. The name is the most important feature of a perfume.
   c. Perfume provides joy and pleasure to customers.
   d. The perfume industry makes promises it can rarely keep.

Reference

2. In line 9, the word *this* refers to _____.
   a. how memories are made
   b. the way smells affect how we feel
   c. the connection between memories and emotions
   d. the idea that people are good at remembering smells

Detail

3. According to Harry Frémont, a good fragrance is a balance between _____.
   a. flower and wood essences
   b. plant and animal essences
   c. rare and very common essences
   d. natural and man-made essences

Vocabulary

4. In line 18, the phrase *run through* is closest in meaning to _____.
   a. use up   b. move into
   c. produce   d. earn

Detail

5. According to the author, in perfume sales, _____.
   a. presentation is everything
   b. presentation should be simple
   c. presentation is as important as the product
   d. presentation is less important than the product

Inference

6. What is probably the main reason the perfumes in the Paris store are so well guarded?
   a. Each bottle is worth over $1,000.
   b. The store has been robbed many times.
   c. It is a way to impress customers.
   d. French stores are normally well guarded.

Detail

7. What does Annie Buzantian suggest people do when buying a perfume?
   a. Try it on before you buy it.
   b. Wear it out at night before you buy it.
   c. Buy different perfumes for different days.
   d. Buy the best perfume that you can afford.

Did You Know?

Civet, an essence derived from material taken from under the tails of civets, has long been valued as an ingredient in perfumes.

Understanding Synonyms

A *synonym* is a word that has the same meaning as, or is very similar to, another word. We often use synonyms to avoid overusing words. Knowledge of a word's synonym(s) greatly increases your vocabulary. It can also help you put ideas into your own words when paraphrasing. When you learn a new word, also list any synonyms you know. For example: *smell = scent = aroma = fragrance*.

If a synonym is slightly different from another word, note the difference: *perfume (for women) = cologne (for men)*.

A. Matching. For each word in *italics*, circle the word that is closest in meaning. Look back at the reading for help.

1. *marketing* (line 4)   a. advertising   b. buying   c. making
2. *connect* (line 5)   a. find   b. sell   c. associate
3. *risky* (line 17)   a. expensive   b. dangerous   c. profitable
4. *hype* (line 31)   a. money   b. material   c. publicity
5. *impression* (line 37)   a. feeling   b. purchase   c. product

> ∧ A stalk of sweet-smelling lilacs

B. Substitution. Read the excerpt from the reading below. Find and replace words in the paragraph with synonyms from the box.

~~cologne~~	every	kind	shop	stylishly	uniquely	well-known

^w
In a Paris ~~perfume~~ store, a building of shining stone, metal, and glass,

famous perfumes are displayed and guarded like works of art in the

nearby Louvre Museum. Salespeople are dressed smartly in black, and

each type of perfume is sold in a distinctively shaped bottle.

Critical Thinking   Discuss with a partner. How is perfume or cologne marketed in your country? What are some ideas usually connected to perfume ads? Are they convincing?

Vocabulary Practice

A. Completion. Complete the information below with the words in the box.

| budget | derived | distinctive | essences | obtain |

In perfume making, **1.** _____ that come from animals are
steadily being replaced by synthetic ones. For many years, a material
known as *ambergris* was used in perfumes. Ambergris comes from inside
certain sperm whales. Perfume companies often **2.** _____ it
from people who find it floating on the ocean or lying on a beach. It has a
very **3.** _____ aroma. Today, ambergris is very expensive and
can often be beyond the **4.** _____ of many perfume makers,
so synthetic essences partly **5.** _____ from plants are used to
create similar aromas.

B. Words in Context. Complete each sentence with the correct answer.

1. If you are asked to **guard** some jewelry, you make sure _____.

   a. nobody steals it   b. you get a good price for it

2. An **authority** on perfume _____.

   a. owns a lot of it   b. knows a lot about it

3. If a ceremony was **preceded** by dinner, the dinner took place ____.

   a. before   b. after

4. If you put **emphasis** on a word when you speak,
the word is probably _____.

   a. very important   b. not important at all

5. When works of art are **displayed** at a museum, _____.

   a. everyone can enjoy them   b. they are kept out of sight

Ambergris is very rare
and can cost up to $20
per gram. Buying and
selling ambergris is illegal
in many countries in order
to protect the endangered
sperm whale.

Word Partnership
Use *obtain* with: (*adj.*) **able to** obtain, **difficult to**
obtain, **easy to** obtain, **unable to** obtain; (*n.*) obtain
approval, obtain **a copy**, obtain **information**.

VIEWING Madagascar Perfume

Before You Watch

A. Discuss. Discuss these questions with a partner.

1. Do you ever wear perfume or cologne? If so, when? If not, why not?
2. Do you have a favorite perfume or cologne? How would you describe it?
3. What is your favorite smell? When or where can you smell it?
4. Is there a particular smell you can't stand?

While You Watch

A. Completion. Look at the pictures and read the captions. Then watch the video. Circle the word or phrase that best completes each caption.

1. This scientist is an authority on the subject of (**plants and animals / scents and tastes**).

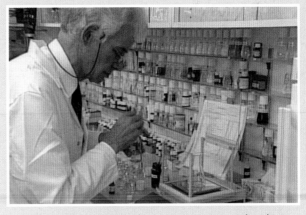

2. In the laboratory, the scientists use technology to (**recreate the scents / create new scents**).

3. The scientists have found two or three types of fruit whose (**smell / taste**) is still unknown.

4. (**Only a few / Many**) of these scents and flavors will be exported to stores all around the world.

After You Watch

A. True or False. Read the sentences below. According to the video, are these statements true (**T**) or false (**F**)?

1. The island of Madagascar is renowned for its distinctive cultures.   **T**   **F**
2. The Swiss scientists hope to find essences for new perfumes.   **T**   **F**
3. The scientists go into the forest and climb up the trees.   **T**   **F**
4. The scents that the scientists find will be used in bath products.   **T**   **F**
5. Chemist Willi Grab was not happy with one flavor he tasted.   **T**   **F**

B. Discuss. Read about the Fragrance Wheel. Then discuss the questions below with a partner.

The **Fragrance Wheel** is a chart used to classify types of fragrances. It allows a retailer to suggest different fragrances in a similar category to the ones a customer prefers. Look at the fragrance categories below.

1. What do you think the things in the pictures smell like? Try to imagine them.
2. What fragrance category do you think you like best? What might this say about you?
3. What category do you like least? Can you explain why?

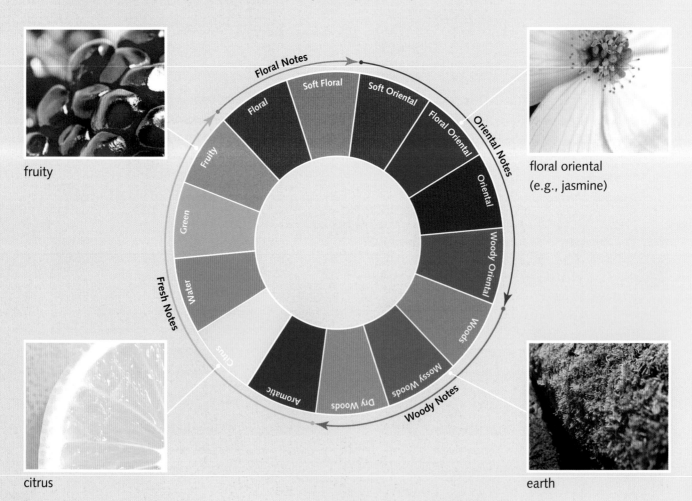

fruity

floral oriental
(e.g., jasmine)

citrus

earth

8

GREAT EXPLORERS

Many early explorers traveled the world by ship, spending months and even years at sea.

Warm Up

Discuss these questions with a partner.

1. Who are some great explorers from history? What are they well known for?

2. Which places remain to be explored today?

3. Would you like to be an explorer? Why or why not?

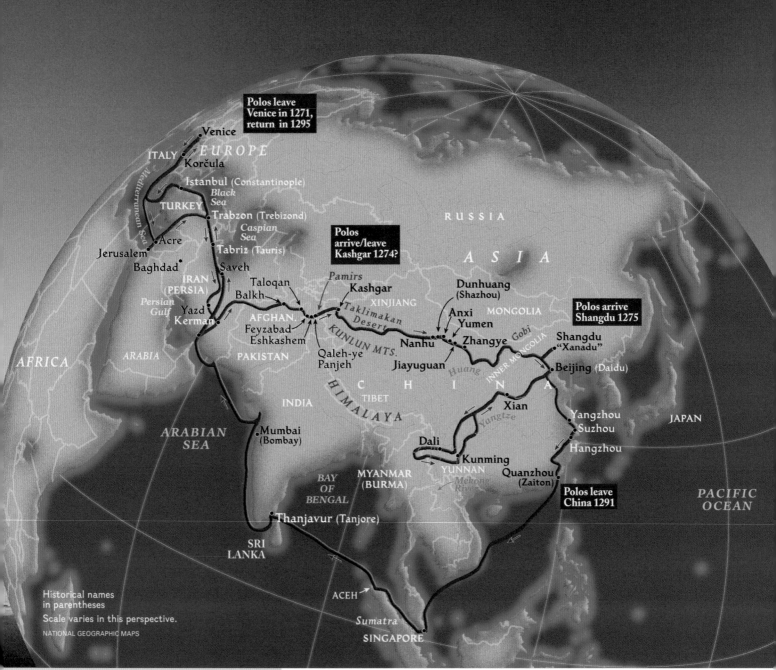

Route map of Marco Polo's journey

The map shows the following labels:

Polos leave Venice in 1271, return in 1295

Venice
ITALY
Korčula
EUROPE
Istanbul (Constantinople)
TURKEY
Black Sea
Trabzon (Trebizond)
Caspian Sea
Acre
Tabriz (Tauris)
Jerusalem
Baghdad
Saveh
IRAN (PERSIA)
Persian Gulf
Yazd
Kerman
AFRICA
ARABIA
AFGHAN.
Feyzabad
Eshkashem
Qaleh-ye Panjeh
PAKISTAN
Taloqan
Balkh
Pamirs
Kashgar
XINJIANG
Taklimakan Desert
KUNLUN MTS.
Nanhu
Jiayuguan
Polos arrive/leave Kashgar 1274?
RUSSIA
ASIA
Dunhuang (Shazhou)
Anxi
Yumen
MONGOLIA
Zhangye
Gobi
INNER MONGOLIA
Shangdu "Xanadu"
Beijing (Daidu)
Polos arrive Shangdu 1275
Huang
CHINA
TIBET
HIMALAYA
INDIA
Mumbai (Bombay)
ARABIAN SEA
Dali
Yangtze
Kunming
YUNNAN
Mekong River
Xian
Yangzhou
Suzhou
Hangzhou
Quanzhou (Zaiton)
JAPAN
PACIFIC OCEAN
Polos leave China 1291
MYANMAR (BURMA)
BAY OF BENGAL
Thanjavur (Tanjore)
SRI LANKA
ACEH
Sumatra
SINGAPORE

Historical names in parentheses
Scale varies in this perspective.
NATIONAL GEOGRAPHIC MAPS

Before You Read

A. Reading Maps. Look at the map of the explorer Marco Polo's journey. Then answer the questions.

1. Where did Marco Polo start and finish his trip? For how many years did he travel?

2. What were some of the furthest places he reached during his travels?

3. What other places did he visit? What do you know about these places?

B. Predict. Why do you think Marco Polo went on such a long journey? Read the passage to check your ideas.

MARCO POLO IN CHINA

In Marco Polo's journal, he writes of the great cities of China, filled with grand buildings and palaces, like nothing he had ever seen before.

1   The Polos—Marco, his father Niccolò, and his uncle Maffeo—had been traveling for three and a half years when they finally achieved their **objective**—a long-awaited meeting with the powerful Mongol leader, Kublai Khan. The

5   historic event took place in 1275 at the Khan's luxurious summer capital[1] in Shengdu, in what is now northern China. Kublai Khan was surprisingly **informal** as he greeted his tired guests: "Welcome, gentlemen! Please stand up. How've you been? How was the trip?"

10   Marco Polo's trip had, in fact, started more than 9,000 kilometers (5,600 miles) away in Venice when he was just

---

1 The **capital** of a country is the city where its government meets.

"Through [this great city] runs a large river . . . The number of boats on this river is so great that no one who should read or hear the tale would believe it . . . In fact, it is so big that it seems to be a sea rather than a river!"
–Marco Polo

a teenager. His father and uncle already knew Kublai Khan from a previous visit five years earlier, when they had spent a short time in Shengdu. On this second trip, the Polos stayed for 17 years before
15 they returned home. They made themselves useful to the Khan and **undertook** various missions[2] and tasks for him. It is likely that the Khan considered it an honor[3] that these Europeans—who were rare in China—had made this extremely difficult journey, and he took the opportunity to make good use of their skills and knowledge.

20 While he was in the service of Kublai Khan, "the most powerful man in people and in lands and in treasure that ever was in the world," Marco Polo was able to learn and experience many things that were new to Europeans. In his travel **journal**, he wrote that Kublai Khan's palace was the greatest he had ever seen. He **admired** the
25 Khan's recently completed new capital, Daidu, whose streets were "so straight and so broad." The city was located in what is now the center of Beijing, and Kublai Khan's city planning can still be **perceived** in the straight, broad streets of China's modern capital.

2 A **mission** is an important task, especially one that involves traveling.

3 Something that is an **honor** is special and desirable.

We learn from Marco Polo that, in the **administration** of his
empire, Kublai Khan made use of a fast and simple message system.
Horse riders spaced every 40 kilometers allowed messages to cover
500 kilometers a day. As soon as one horse had run 40 kilometers,
the next horse would run the next 40 kilometers, and so on. Marco
also learned the secret of asbestos cloth, which is made from a
mineral and doesn't catch fire. Paper money also took him by
surprise, since it was not yet in use in the West at that time. Homes
were heated with "black stones . . . which burn like logs." Those
stones were coal—unknown in most of Europe—and were so
plentiful that many people had a hot bath three times a week.

Although the Khan did not want his visitors to leave, the Polos
finally received permission to return home in 1292. Marco
continued his observations while on the ocean **voyage** by way
of Sumatra and India. After he returned home, Marco completed
a book about his trip, full of details about his amazing cultural
experiences. It was probably the single greatest **contribution** to
geographical knowledge ever made to the West about the East.

Marco Polo wrote that he saw 15,000 boats a day sailing on the nearby Yangtze River. The river is famous for its beauty, trade, and influence on art and culture. Today, the lights of boats shine on the Qinhuaihe, a branch of the Yangtze River flowing through the city of Nanjing.

Multiple Choice. Choose the best answer for each question.

Gist

1. What is the passage mainly about?
   a. Marco Polo's relationship with Kublai Khan
   b. why Marco Polo's travels are important
   c. why Marco Polo decided to write a book
   d. how Marco Polo was able to reach China

Detail

2. What was surprising about the Polos' meeting with the Khan?
   a. He could speak English.
   b. He spoke to them informally.
   c. He lived in a luxurious palace.
   d. He didn't remember them from a previous visit.

Detail

3. The phrase *considered it an honor* in line 17 is closest to _____.
   a. was angry   b. thought it was strange
   c. felt respected   d. thought it was useful

Detail

4. Kublai Khan used _____ to deliver messages to his people.
   a. runners   b. the Polos
   c. horse riders   d. birds

Inference

5. Marco Polo saw that asbestos cloth, paper money, and coal were used in the East. According to the passage, this shows that _____.
   a. the West already knew about and used these inventions
   b. the East had learned various technologies from the West
   c. the West had forgotten the technologies used in the East
   d. the East was ahead of the West in some areas of technology

Sequence

6. What did Marco Polo do after he left China but before he returned to Venice?
   a. He wrote a book.
   b. He crossed Asia by land.
   c. He visited India and Sumatra.
   d. He undertook a mission for Kublai Khan.

Reference

7. In line 45, the word *it* refers to _____.
   a. culture   b. the book
   c. completion   d. his contribution

Did You Know?

Some people believe Marco Polo introduced pasta to Europe from China. He does mention "macaroni or other sorts of pasta" in his journal. However, Europeans had probably known about these foods for many years.

Understanding Time Clauses/ Time Relationships

In addition to *before* and *after*, we can also indicate time relationships with *when*, *as soon as*, *as*, and *while*. These words can begin a sentence (with a comma following the clause), or be used in the middle of a sentence.

The word *when* can be used when one action happens after another action, or during the same period of time.

Example 1: *When I decided to take a trip to China, I told my parents.*
Example 2: *When he was six, he moved to another city.*

Use *as soon as* when one action happens immediately after another action.

Example: *As soon as I landed in Beijing, I texted my parents.*

Use *while* and *as* when two actions happen at the same time.

Example 1: *I felt very excited as the taxi arrived at my hotel.*
Example 2: *I made a lot of new friends while I was in China.*

A. Noticing. Find and underline the words *before*, *after*, *when*, *as soon as*, *as*, and *while* in the passage on pages 117–119.

B. Sequencing. For each pair of actions, mark them **1** (happened first) or **2** (happened second). If both actions happened at the same time, mark both **1**.

1. _____ Marco Polo met Kublai Khan.
   _____ Marco Polo traveled for three and a half years.

2. _____ Marco Polo's trip started.
   _____ Marco Polo became a teenager.

3. _____ Marco Polo was in the service of Kublai Khan.
   _____ Marco Polo was able to learn and experience many new things.

4. _____ Marco Polo was on an ocean voyage.
   _____ Marco Polo continued his observations.

5. _____ Marco Polo returned home.
   _____ Marco Polo completed a book.

Critical Thinking Discuss with a partner. Who do you think gained more from the Polos' visit to China—Marco Polo or Kublai Khan? Why?

∧ Marco Polo

Vocabulary Practice

A. Definitions. Complete the definitions using the correct words from the box.

administration admire informal mineral objective undertake

1. Your _____ is what you are trying to achieve.
2. If you _____ someone, you like and respect him or her.
3. A(n) _____ is a solid, naturally occurring substance.
4. When you _____ a task or job, you start doing it.
5. The _____ of a country is conducted by its government.
6. If a situation is _____, it is usually relaxed, friendly, or unofficial.

B. Completion. Choose the correct words to complete the information below.

After surviving the dangers of the ocean **1. (voyage / mineral)** from
China, Marco Polo reached his home city of Venice. But more troubles
waited for him there. Italy at that time was not united under one
government, and the **2. (administration / admiration)** of each city was
left to different powerful families. So the different cities were often at
war with each other. During fighting between Venice and Genoa, Marco
Polo was put in prison. There, he met Rustichello, a writer of fairy tales,
who **3. (undertook / contributed)** to Polo's future fame by helping him
create a(n) **4. (journal / objective)** of his travels. Because of this book,
many people around the world **5. (perceive / admire)** Polo's achievements
as an explorer. Today, Marco Polo is **6. (perceived / contributed)** by many
to be one of the greatest explorers that ever lived.

> **Word Partnership**
> Use **undertake** with: (*n.*) undertake
> **an action**, undertake **a project**,
> undertake **a task**.

Marco Polo completed his
journal for "all people who
wish to know . . . the different
regions of the world."

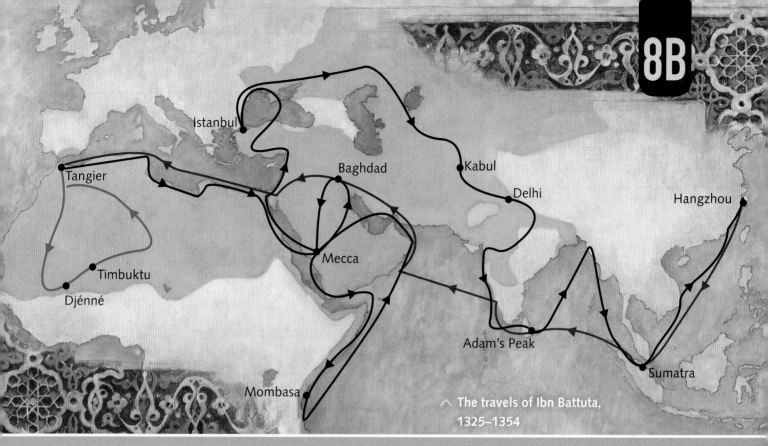

The travels of Ibn Battuta, 1325–1354

Islamic Lands, 14th Century

▶ Route from Tangier to China

▶ Return route

▶ Round trip in Sahara

THE TRAVELS OF IBN BATTUTA

Before You Read

A. Reading Maps. Ibn Battuta was born in Tangier, in what is now Morocco. He was a great explorer, and traveled to many places around the world during the 14th century. Look at the map of his travels, and try to guess the answers to these questions.

1. Who traveled further, Ibn Battuta or Marco Polo?

2. How many places did Ibn Battuta visit?

3. For how many years was Ibn Battuta traveling?

B. Scan. Now quickly read the first two paragraphs on page 124 to check your guesses.

During 30 years of travel, Ibn Battuta visited the furthest edges of the Islamic world—from the deserts of North Africa to China and back.

The Long Journey

"I left Tangier, my birthplace, the 13th of June, 1325, with the **intention** of making the pilgrimage[1] [to Mecca]. . . . to leave all my friends both female and male, to **abandon** my home as birds abandon their nests." So begins
5 an old manuscript[2] in a library in Paris, the travel journal of Ibn Battuta.

Almost two centuries before Columbus, this young Moroccan set off for Mecca. Returning home three decades later, he is now regarded as one of history's great travelers. Driven by curiosity, he journeyed to **remote** corners of the Islamic world, traveling three times as far as Marco Polo,
10 through 44 modern countries. Though little celebrated in the West, his name is well known among Arabs. In his hometown of Tangier, a square, a hotel, a café, a ferry boat, and even a hamburger are named after him.

Prior to his adventures traveling the world, Ibn Battuta studied in Mecca for several years. However, the urge to travel soon took over. He traveled
15 to India, seeking profitable employment with the Sultan[3] of Delhi. On the way, he described his group being attacked in the open country by 80 foot soldiers and two horsemen: "we fought . . . killing one of their horsemen

---

1 A **pilgrimage** is a trip to a place of religious importance.

2 A **manuscript** is a piece of writing that is handwritten, or an early version of a book.

3 A **sultan** is a ruler in some Islamic countries.

After his great journey, Ibn Battuta (center) returned home. He died in 1369 at the age of 64 near the town of Fez. The location of his burial site remains a mystery.

and about twelve of the foot soldiers. . . . I was hit by an arrow and my horse by another, but God in his grace preserved me. . . . We carried the
20 heads of the slain[4] to the castle of Abu Bak'har . . . and suspended[5] them from the wall."

In Delhi, the sultan gave him the position of judge, based on his studies at Mecca. But the sultan had an unpredictable character, and Ibn Battuta was soon looking for an opportunity to leave. When the sultan offered to
25 **finance** a trip to China, Ibn Battuta agreed. He set off in three ships, but **misfortune** struck while he was still on shore. A sudden storm grounded and broke up two ships. Scattering[6] treasure, the storm drowned many people and horses. As he watched, the third ship, with all his belongings and slaves—one carrying his child—was carried out to sea and never
30 heard from again.

After a lifetime of incredible adventures, Ibn Battuta was finally ordered by the Sultan of Morocco to return home to share his **wisdom** with the world. Fortunately, he **consented** and wrote a book that has been **translated** into numerous languages, allowing people everywhere to read
35 about his **unparalleled** journeys.

---

4 Someone who has been **slain** has been killed.

5 If you **suspend** something from a high place, you hang it from that place.

6 If things are **scattered**, they have been thrown or dropped so they are spread all over an area.

Reading Comprehension

Multiple Choice. Choose the best answer for each question.

Gist

1. What is the passage mainly about?
   a. Ibn Battuta's visit to Mecca
   b. Ibn Battuta's character
   c. the adventures of Ibn Battuta
   d. the books that Ibn Battuta wrote

Detail

2. Why did Ibn Battuta first leave Tangier?
   a. to teach
   b. to help his family
   c. to visit Mecca
   d. to look for a job abroad

Vocabulary

3. Which of the following is closest in meaning to the phrase *set off for* in line 6?
   a. arrived at
   b. discussed
   c. left to go to
   d. decided upon

Detail

4. The Sultan of Delhi gave Ibn Battuta the position of judge because _____.
   a. the sultan needed a translator
   b. Ibn Battuta had studied in Mecca
   c. Ibn Battuta had been a judge before
   d. Ibn Battuta had traveled to many countries

Reference

5. What does the word *one* refer to in line 29?
   a. a ship
   b. a storm
   c. a slave
   d. a mother

Detail

6. Why did Ibn Battuta finally return home?
   a. He was tired of traveling.
   b. He feared the Sultan of Delhi.
   c. He didn't have any more money.
   d. The Sultan of Morocco asked him to return.

Inference

7. The writer of this passage most likely thinks that Ibn Battuta's journey _____.
   a. didn't really happen
   b. was inspired by Marco Polo's travels
   c. was common for people of that time
   d. should be more well known in the West today

Did You Know?

In Dubai, there is a large shopping mall named after Ibn Battuta. It has six sections named after areas of the world he visited.

Recognizing Participle Clauses

Participle clauses are very common in written English. They show relationships between two or more actions. Recognizing them will help you understand how one action is related to another action.

Participle clauses can use the present participle (-*ing*) or past participle (-*ed*). When the sentence shows one subject performing two different actions, use the -*ing* form for the first verb.

Example: *She stared at the map. She looked for a bus stop. = Staring at the map, she looked for a bus stop.*

You should use the -*ed* form when one action is in the passive voice.

Example: *The residents were rescued by the firefighters. They all survived the fire. = Rescued by the firefighters, the residents all survived the fire.*

A. Analyzing. These sentences are from the reading on pages 124–125. Choose the correct participle to complete each sentence. Then check your answers in the reading.

1. (**Returning / Returned**) home three decades later, he is now regarded as one of history's great travelers. (paragraph 2)

2. (**Driving / Driven**) by curiosity, he journeyed to remote corners of the Islamic world . . . (paragraph 2)

3. Though little (**celebrating / celebrated**) in the West, his name is well known among Arabs. (paragraph 2)

4. He traveled to India, (**seeking / sought**) profitable employment with the Sultan of Delhi. (paragraph 3)

5. (**Scattering / Scattered**) treasure, the storm drowned many people and horses. (paragraph 4)

B. Combining. Combine the two sentences into one. Make the first sentence a participle clause.

1. Ibn Battuta left his friends behind. Ibn Battuta started traveling in 1325.

   _____

2. Ibn Battuta's book is known as *Rihla*. His book details his travels in Asia and Africa. _____

Critical Thinking Discuss with a partner. How were the travels of Marco Polo and Ibn Battuta different? How were they similar?

Vocabulary Practice

A. Definitions. Read the information below. Then complete the definitions using the words in **red**.

> During his travels, Ibn Battuta suffered many **misfortunes**. Here's one: In his final journey, he traveled to the **remote** land of Mali, with the **intention** of meeting a king who gave his visitors wonderful gifts. Said to be **unparalleled**, these gifts often included large amounts of gold. However, **prior** to Ibn Battuta's arrival, the old king died. The new king, Mansa Sulayman, only gave Ibn Battuta a little food. When he saw his gift, Ibn Battuta could only laugh.

1. An area that is _____ is far away and difficult to get to.

2. If you have the _____ of doing something, you have decided to do it.

3. A person's _____ are bad or unlucky things that happen to them.

4. If something happens _____ to another thing, it happens before it.

5. If you describe something as _____, you are emphasizing that it is bigger, better, or worse than anything else of its kind.

B. Completion. Complete the sentences below with the words in the box.

abandoned   consented   financed   translators   wisdom

1. Thanks to the work of many _____, the writings of Ibn Battuta can be read in all major languages.

2. The king and queen of Spain _____ Christopher Columbus's voyage to the New World.

3. Kublai Khan finally _____ to the Polos' request to return to Europe.

4. A good king is one who has great _____ and makes good decisions for his people.

5. Urban explorers explore places within a city, including buildings that have been _____ and now lie empty.

> **Thesaurus**
> **remote** Also look up:
> (*adj.*) *faraway, distant*

The king of Mali, Mansa Sulayman >

VIEWING The Legend of Marco Polo

Before You Watch

A. Definitions. Here are some words you will hear in the video. Match the words to their definitions.

1. formidable •
2. banquet •
3. excavate •
4. province •

• a. an area within a country
• b. to remove earth carefully to find buried objects
• c. a large, grand meal, usually for many people
• d. inspiring fear or respect by being large or powerful

∧ The Polos leave Venice for their travels to the Far East.

While You Watch

A. Completion. Many people believe Marco Polo visited China, but others argue that he didn't. As you watch, choose the correct words from the video to complete the chart.

Arguments against Polo visiting China	Arguments for Polo visiting China
There are factual **1. (statements / inaccuracies)** in Polo's book, such as saying a **2. (battle / wedding)** took place in the wrong year.	There are details in his book that couldn't have been **5. (invented / believed)** in Europe, such as Polo seeing **6. (camels / coal)** for the first time.
The book describes things that are not possible, such as a **3. (tiger / fish)** that is a hundred feet long with **4. (feathers / fur)** on it.	Polo described a hall big enough for **7. (6,000 / 10,000)** people. When the city was excavated, the placement and style of the **8. (buildings / streets)** were exactly as Polo had described them.

After You Watch

A. Correction. The captions below are not accurate. Use the information in the video to correct each caption.

1. When Marco Polo wrote his book, he was in jail in China.

_____

_____

2. Marco Polo set off for China from Venice in 1271 A.D., traveling as a geographer.

_____

_____

3. The Chinese call the Taklamakan Desert the "desert of summer."

_____

_____

4. Marco Polo claims he went to Shengdu, to Kublai Khan's spring palace.

_____

_____

B. Discuss. Discuss these questions with a partner.

1. Which arguments do you think are stronger—that Marco Polo did or didn't visit China?

2. Is there information in this video that supports or doesn't agree with the reading on pages 117–119? If so, which do you think is more convincing?

9

A young Sami woman
from Jokkmokk, Sweden

WHO WE ARE

Warm Up

Discuss these questions with a partner.

1. Do you look like the person in the picture? If not, how are you different? How would you describe yourself?

2. What makes you similar to or different from your parents?

3. How are you different now from when you were younger?

Before You Read

A. Completion. Look at the picture and read the caption. Then complete the sentences below using the correct form of the words in **bold**.

1. When someone begins a sentence with "_____," usually something bad has happened.

2. To _____ to take a test, people usually spend time studying for it.

3. If you _____ something, you try to find it.

4. The period during which children gradually become adults is called _____.

5. One way to _____ is to go to a party and meet people.

B. Predict. At what age do you think a person's brain has finished developing? Read the passage and check your ideas.

⌃ During **adolescence**, most teens **hunt for** new experiences and opportunities to **socialize** with new people. **Unfortunately**, teens sometimes go too far and put themselves in danger. But science now suggests these experiences help **prepare** teens for adult life.

THE TEENAGE BRAIN

1   Parents, teachers, and others who **deal** closely **with** teenagers know how difficult the adolescent years can be. Adolescents have always been known to do wild,[1] even dangerous, things. This was thought to be due to the "foolishness[2] of youth." Now,

5   brain-imaging technology allows scientists to study the physical development of the brain in more detail than ever before. Their discoveries have led to a new theory of why teens act this way.

A Work in Progress

  Recently, scientists discovered that though our brains are

10   almost at their full size by the age of six, they are far from fully developed. Only during adolescence do our brains truly "grow up." During this time, they go through great changes, like a computer system being upgraded.[3] This "upgrade" was once thought to be finished by about age 12. Now, scientists have

15   **concluded** that our brains continue to change until age 25. Such changes make us better at balancing **impulses** with following rules. But a still-developing brain does this **clumsily**. The result, scientists claim, is the unpredictable behavior seen in teenagers.

1 **Wild** behavior is uncontrolled, excited, or energetic.

2 **Foolishness** is the opposite of wisdom, and refers to the behavior of someone who makes bad decisions.

3 When a machine gets **upgraded**, it gets improved.

Pleasure Seekers

20　The studies confirm that teens are more likely to take **risks** and behave in extreme ways. Fortunately, the news isn't all negative. As brain scientist B. J. Casey points out, the teen brain inspires such behavior in order to help teens prepare for adult life.

One way the brain does this is by changing the way teens measure
25　risk and **reward**. Researchers found that when teens think about rewards, their brains **release** more of the chemicals that create **pleasure** than an adult brain would. Researchers believe this makes the rewards seem more important than the risks, and makes teens feel the excitement of new experiences more keenly than adults do.

30　Research into the structure of the teen brain also found that it makes social connections seem especially rewarding. As such, teens have an **intense** need to meet new people. Scientists suggest this is because as teens, we begin to **realize** our peers may one day control the world we live in. Because it is still developing, a teen brain can change
35　to deal with new situations. So, it connects social rewards with even more pleasure. In this way, the brain encourages teens to have a wide circle of friends, which is believed to make us more successful in life.

Unfortunately, this hunt for greater rewards can sometimes lead teens to make bad decisions. However, it also means that teens are more
40　likely, and less afraid, to try new things or to be independent. The scientists' findings suggest that in the long run, the impulses of the teen brain are what help teens leave their parents' care and live their own lives successfully.

⌃ For teens, building friendships and making new friends are especially rewarding activities.

Reading Comprehension

Multiple Choice. Choose the best answer for each question.

Cohesion

1. The following sentence would best be placed at the end of which paragraph? *So teens are always searching for an experience that is more exciting than the last.*
   - a. paragraph 1
   - b. paragraph 2
   - c. paragraph 4
   - d. paragraph 5

Detail

2. Which of these statements about an adolescent's brain is NOT true?
   - a. It is almost at its full size.
   - b. It is going through a lot of changes.
   - c. It does some things in a clumsy way.
   - d. It is better than an adult brain at following rules.

Paraphrase

3. What does the author mean by the phrase *the news isn't all negative* (line 21)?
   - a. Many teenagers are able to change their behavior.
   - b. The negative side of the research is not understood.
   - c. The way the teen brain works has some advantages.
   - d. The impulses of a teenage brain should be controlled.

Vocabulary

4. What do the words *more keenly* mean in line 29?
   - a. more strongly
   - b. more loudly
   - c. more slowly
   - d. more strangely

Cause and Effect

5. What leads teens to meet new people?
   - a. the fear of being alone
   - b. the need to control others
   - c. the desire to leave home sooner
   - d. the excitement of new experiences

Cause and Effect

6. What could happen if a teenager doesn't socialize?
   - a. The teen's brain may stop developing.
   - b. The teen's brain may develop badly.
   - c. The teen may not take as many risks.
   - d. The teen may miss contacts needed for future success.

Main Idea

7. Which of the following would be the best heading for the last paragraph?
   - a. A Finished Brain
   - b. The Rewards of Friendship
   - c. The Parents' Role
   - d. How a Teen Makes Friends

Did You Know?

To a teen, it may make sense to stay up late, but to stay healthy, teenagers need between 9 and 10 hours of sleep a night.

Evaluating Claims

Many articles and scientific texts cite research or expert opinions to support claims put forth by the writer. One way to evaluate the strength of a claim is to look closely at the verbs used. Verbs such as *find (out)*, *point out*, *know*, *discover*, and *conclude* show a high degree of confidence in the claims being presented. Verbs such as *suggest*, *think*, *believe*, and *claim* show a lower degree of confidence.

A. Noticing. Look back at the passage on pages 133–134. Find and underline the claims below.

1. A person's brain reaches almost its full size by the age of six.

2. The brain goes through a process of great changes which actually continues until age 25.

3. The result of a still-developing and clumsy brain is the unpredictable behavior seen in teenagers.

4. Teens are more likely to take risks and behave in extreme ways.

5. The teen brain makes rewards seem more important than risks, and teens feel new experiences more keenly.

6. In the long run, the impulses of the teen brain are what help teens live their own lives successfully.

B. Evaluating Claims. Identify and write the verbs in the passage that are used to make the claims in **A**. Then mark each claim as showing a high (**H**) degree or a lower (**L**) degree of confidence.

1. <u>discovered</u>   H   L

2. _____   H   L

3. _____   H   L

4. _____   H   L

5. _____   H   L

6. _____   H   L

∧ On Sundays, in Tokyo's Harajuku area, teens like this girl gather, dressed in the latest street fashions.

Critical Thinking Discuss with a partner. What do you think is the biggest difference between being a teenager and being an adult?

Vocabulary Practice

A. Completion. Circle the correct words or phrases to complete the information below.

Psychologist Laurence Steinberg has found that the biggest **1. (reward / risk)** takers are 14- to 17-year-olds. This is not because they don't **2. (realize / release)** certain activities are dangerous but because they value the **3. (rewards / conclusions)** more than the risks. Steinberg uses a driving video game to test this idea. In this **4. (impulsive / intense)** game, the driver controls the speed of a car. Players have to **5. (release / deal with)** traffic lights that change quickly from green to yellow to red, forcing quick go-or-stop decisions. The study showed Steinberg that when a friend was watching, teens took twice as many **6. (risks / impulses)** as when they played alone. From this, Steinberg **7. (dealt with / concluded)** that social rewards can lead teens to take more risks.

∧ Most traffic lights have red (stop), yellow (slow down), and green (go) lights.

B. Words in Context. Complete each sentence with the correct answer.

1. If someone is **clumsy**, they are likely to _____.
   a. handle things with care   b. break something

2. If someone has an **impulse** to jump into a lake, they have
   _____.
   a. a great fear of it   b. a sudden desire to do it

3. Something that gives many people **pleasure** is _____.
   a. listening to music   b. taking exams

4. When you **realize** something, you _____.
   a. become aware of it   b. choose not to think about it

5. If you **release** an animal, you _____.
   a. catch it   b. let it go

6. An example of an **intense** experience would be _____.
   a. a ride in a race car   b. a dinner with friends

> **Word Partnership**
> Use **reward** with:
> (*v.*) **earn** a reward,
> **promise** a reward,
> **deserve** a reward; (*n.*)
> reward **excellence**,
> reward **loyalty**; (*adj.*)
> **financial** reward,
> **considerable** reward.

Seeing DOUBLE

Before You Read

Identical twins, like the Scott twins pictured above, have exactly the same **genes**. This explains the physical features they have **in common**. But some scientists studying twins have concluded that genes can also **influence** personality, and even **IQ**.

A. Completion. Look at the picture and read the caption. Then complete the sentences below using the words in **bold**.

1. If your friends have things _____, they are the same in some way.

2. If something can _____ you, it can affect your feelings or behavior.

3. A person's _____ is a number that represents their intelligence, based on their score on a special test.

4. If two things are exactly the same, we say they are _____.

5. The growth of our bodies follows a plan contained in our _____.

B. Predict. The Jim Twins, in the passage on page 139, were separated as babies but met aged 39. Try to guess some things they had in common. Then read the passage to check your ideas.

Gene Theory

Many scientists once believed that physical similarities between identical twins are **genetic**, while their personalities, intelligence, and other differences between them are an effect of their environment. Now scientists are discovering that the **boundaries** between genetics and environment are not so clear.

The Jim Twins

Identical twins Jim Springer and Jim Lewis were **adopted** as babies and **raised** by different couples. When the Jims finally met at age 39, they discovered they had plenty in common. Both were six feet tall, 180 pounds. They had the same smile and the same voice. When psychologist Thomas Bouchard Jr. invited the Jim twins to his lab, his **colleagues** found it very hard to **tell** them **apart**.

But the similarities didn't stop at the physical. They'd both had dogs named Toy. They had both married women named Linda, and then **divorced** them. They'd both been sheriffs,[1] enjoyed carpentry,[2] suffered **severe** headaches, and **admitted** to leaving love notes around the house for their wives. They had so much in common, it seemed unlikely these were just **coincidences**.

^ Placed side by side (Lewis on the left, Springer on the right), the Jim twins' faces are so alike that they seem to make a single face.

Genetics and Intelligence

The Jim twins were just one of 137 sets of separated twins Bouchard tested. When they compared the twins' IQ scores, Bouchard and his team reached a surprising conclusion. They concluded that intelligence was mostly connected to genetics rather than to training or education. It seemed the differences in family and environment had little effect.

However, genes can't control everything, argues geneticist Danielle Reed, who also studies twins. Reed's research shows that though nothing can truly change our DNA, environmental differences that a child experiences before birth and in their first year can sometimes affect the way the DNA behaves, making even identical twins into very different people. "What I like to say is that Mother Nature[3] writes some things in pencil and some things in pen," she explains. "Things written in pen you can't change. That's DNA. But things written in pencil you can."

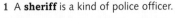

1 A **sheriff** is a kind of police officer.
2 **Carpentry** is the activity of making and repairing wooden things.
3 **Mother Nature** is sometimes used to refer to nature, especially when it is being considered as a force that affects human beings.

Reading Comprehension

Multiple Choice. Choose the best answer for each question.

Gist

1. What is the passage mainly about?
   a. how identical twins are formed
   b. the effects genes have on personality
   c. the differences between identical twins
   d. the connection between male vs. female twins

Detail

2. In the past, scientists believed that _____.
   a. genetics controlled some parts of who we are
   b. genetics controlled everything about who we are
   c. environment played an important part in how twins look
   d. our genes are affected by the environment around us

Main Idea

3. Which heading could best replace "The Jim Twins"?
   a. Finding Lost Twins   b. What Makes Twins Different
   c. The Sad Separated Twins   d. More Similar than Different

Vocabulary

4. The phrase *didn't stop at* in line 15 is closest in meaning
   to _____.
   a. went beyond   b. passed quickly by
   c. changed more than   d. had nothing to do with

Reference

5. Who does the word *they* refer to in line 23?
   a. the Jim Twins   b. sets of twins
   c. Bouchard and twins   d. Bouchard and his team

Detail

6. According to Bouchard and his team, what is intelligence
   mostly related to?
   a. genetics   b. training
   c. education   d. parenting

Paraphrase

7. What does Danielle Reed mean by her statement, *"Things written in pen you can't change. That's DNA. But things written in pencil you can."* in lines 35–36?
   a. The environment can change your DNA.
   b. The way your DNA affects you can change.
   c. You can change anything if you try hard enough.
   d. You cannot change things that are controlled by DNA.

Did You Know?

Identical twins share the same DNA but do not have the same fingerprints.

Reading Skill

Understanding Inference

A reading text does not always state everything directly. Sometimes you need to "read between the lines" to find the meaning. You can infer meaning by using your knowledge of the topic, clues and hints in the text, and common sense. An inference is a kind of "smart guess."

We make inferences every day. For example, if someone enters a room shaking a wet umbrella, we can infer that it is raining outside, even though we don't actually see the rain. Making inferences while reading allows the reader to reach a deeper level of meaning.

Identical twins, like these young surfers, often share hobbies.

A. Inference. Look back at paragraphs 2–3 of the passage on page 139. Then read the sentences below. Can you infer the information below from the information given in the passage? Circle **Yes** or **No**.

1. They both like dogs.   **Yes**   **No**
2. They both have sons, but no daughters.   **Yes**   **No**
3. They both believe keeping the law is important.   **Yes**   **No**
4. They frequently had to go to the hospital.   **Yes**   **No**
5. They are both romantic husbands.   **Yes**   **No**

B. Inference. Look back at the passage. Answer the questions.

1. In Bouchard's study, each of the people tested _____.

    a. looked exactly like their twin
    b. had the same kind of job as their twin
    c. had about the same IQ level as their twin

2. What statement would Danielle Reed probably agree with?

    a. Only DNA affects a person's development.
    b. Identical twins always have identical personalities.
    c. It's possible to change some things about yourself.

Critical Thinking Discuss with a partner. What are some challenges twins might face? What challenges might their parents face?

Vocabulary Practice

A. Completion. Complete the information below with words in the box. One word is extra.

admitted	adopted	apart	boundaries	coincidences	raised

One day, Samantha Futerman, an actress in the U.S., received a Facebook message that would change her life. The message was from Anais Bordier, a young woman from France. Anais asked Samantha when she was born. She **1.** _____ to Samantha that she had been **2.** _____ as a baby, and thought Samantha could be her twin. To Samantha's surprise, Anais looked just like her. In fact, it was almost impossible to tell them **3.** _____. The young women found out that they had been born on the same date in the same town in South Korea, and had very similar personalities. To confirm that these weren't just **4.** _____, they took DNA tests, which concluded that they were identical twins. **5.** _____ by different families in different countries, neither had known she had a sister.

∧ Samantha Futerman (pictured above) and Anais met for the first time in 2013, and are making a movie about their experience.

B. Words in Context. Complete each sentence with the correct answer.

1. If a disease is **genetic**, _____ are likely to have it.
   a. people who live near you   b. other people in your family

2. If you have a **severe** pain in your leg, it hurts _____.
   a. a lot   b. a little

3. The **boundaries** of a country are at the _____ of that country's land.
   a. end   b. center

4. Two people who are **divorced** are no longer _____.
   a. planning to get married   b. married

5. If you can **tell** two people **apart**, you can recognize their _____.
   a. similarities   b. differences

6. Your **colleagues** are people you _____ with.
   a. live   b. work

> **Thesaurus**
> **severe** Also look up: (*adj.*) *serious, harsh, intense, drastic, extreme, tough*

VIEWING The Global Village

Before You Watch

A. Warm Up. Read about the Genographic Project. Then discuss the questions below with a partner.

Since 2005, the National Geographic Society's Genographic Project has worked to answer important questions about who we are as human beings, like: *Where did humans come from? How did we come to live all over the Earth?* The project collects DNA from people all around the world and studies it to see what DNA has been passed down from their ancestors. The results provide valuable information about our past.

1. What do you think the people in the picture are doing?
2. Where do you think people in your country originally came from?
3. What could be some benefits of learning more about our past from our DNA?

While You Watch

A. Viewing. The video shows a gathering of some Genographic Project participants in New York. As you watch, check (✓) the topics the video discusses.

☐ the number of participants that attended

☐ the different groups people are divided into

☐ why people move from one place to another

☐ the continent where we all came from

☐ where humans have spent most of our history

After You Watch

A. Completion. Complete the sentences below with the correct numbers and words in the box. Not all the numbers and words are used.

14,000	25,000	40,000	45,000	50,000	60,000
Africa	Central Asia	Europe	the Middle East	North America	

1. People moved into the Americas _____ years ago and into _____ 35,000 years ago.

2. Both groups who moved to the Americas and Europe came from _____. They began to live there _____ years ago.

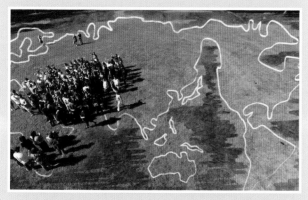

3. People in East and South Asia lived there _____ years ago. They came from _____ 50,000 years ago.

4. Everybody in the world originally came from _____. Humans first left there _____ years ago.

B. Discuss. Discuss these questions with a partner.

1. Would you participate in the Genographic Project? Why or why not?

2. One participant said about the project, "We're one family with all the problems involved in family relationships, but one big family." What do you think she meant?

10

GLOBAL WARMING

Water pours into the sea from a river of melted ice on Negribreen, a glacier in Norway.

Warm Up

Discuss these questions with a partner.

1. Do you think people in your country are worried about global warming?

2. What parts of the world do you think are most affected by global warming?

3. What changes do you think could occur if the world continues to get warmer?

145

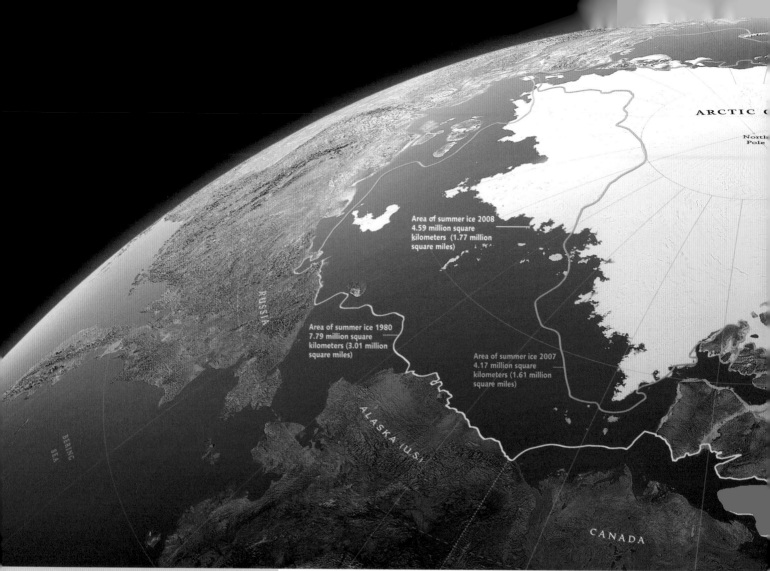

Area of summer ice 2008
4.59 million square
kilometers (1.77 million
square miles)

Area of summer ice 1980
7.79 million square
kilometers (3.01 million
square miles)

Area of summer ice 2007
4.17 million square
kilometers (1.61 million
square miles)

RUSSIA

BERING
SEA

ALASKA (U.S.)

CANADA

ARCTIC O

North
Pole

Before You Read

A. Reading Maps. Look at the map of the Arctic. Use the information to
complete the text below.

> Rising temperatures can cause changes to our planet. These changes
> are most visible in the Arctic, where a large area of sea is usually
> covered by ice. In 1980, scientists recorded that the Arctic's sea ice in
> summer covered **1.** _____ million square kilometers (km²). By
> 2007, the area of sea ice had dropped to **2.** _____ million km².
> The ice came back a little (to 4.59 million km²) in **3.** _____. But
> by 2012, it had dropped even more, covering only 3.41 million km².

Discuss your answers with a partner. What do you think the map looks like
now? What do you think it will look like in 2050?

B. Scan. The map above also shows the effects of global warming on great
rivers of ice called *glaciers*. When the glaciers are warmed, they move and
melt into the ocean. Scan pages 147–149. Find the names of two glaciers
mentioned in the reading passage.

THE BIG THAW

Area of glacier melt 1980   Area of glacier melt 2007

1   The Chacaltaya ski area sits upon a small mountain glacier in Bolivia. Although the area is less than a kilometer long, it once **hosted** international ski competitions. In the past ten years, however, the snow has melted very quickly. As
5   Chacaltaya glacier melts, dark rocks are uncovered. These rocks **absorb** more heat, causing the snow to melt faster. The cycle seems **unstoppable** in the long run. Today, the snow is almost gone, and so are Chacaltaya's days as a popular ski resort.

A Global Problem

In recent years, scientists all around the world have come to a terrifying conclusion. Global warming is a real problem, and one largely caused by human activity. But as experts debate how to solve the problem, ice in mountains such as
15   Chacaltaya, and near the North and South Poles, is melting faster than even the most pessimistic[1] environmentalists once

⌃ A *thaw* happens when something frozen warms and melts. Most scientists agree global warming is causing the Earth's great areas of ice and snow to do just that.

1 Someone who is **pessimistic** thinks that bad things are going to happen.

feared. Ten years ago, scientists warned that the Arctic Ocean could lose all its ice in about a hundred years. Now, they think it could happen much sooner. As climate scientist Mark Serreze puts
20 it, "Reality is **exceeding** expectations."

Glacier Run

The ice sheet of Greenland is also melting more quickly than scientists predicted. Its largest outlet glacier,[2] Jakobshavn Isbræ, is moving toward the sea faster than expected. In fact, the glacier
25 is moving twice as fast as it was in 1995. Rising air and sea temperatures are two well-known causes. Researchers have also discovered other **unexpected** processes that cause them to melt faster. For instance, water from melting ice runs down **cracks** in the glacier and gets between the ice and the rock below. This
30 makes it easier for the glacier to **slide** into the warmer sea water.

Some researchers believe that Greenland's melting, if it continues, could add at least a meter to global sea levels by 2100. If the ice sheet of Antarctica, now largely unaffected, begins to melt, the next few centuries could see at least a two-meter rise in sea levels,
35 forcing tens of millions of people out of their homes.

Drying Out

While the melting of glaciers may flood some areas of the Earth, global warming is making the water disappear from other places. Many scientists think the glaciers of the Himalayas and the Andes
40 could disappear in this century. As a result, millions of people in India, Bangladesh, Bolivia, and Peru who depend on water from mountain glaciers like Chacaltaya could find themselves in a **critical** situation. An increasing number of heat waves and droughts worldwide also suggests global warming is having an
45 impact on humans right now, and that it could change the face of the world in the future.

How can we avoid these terrible **consequences**? "We have to have a serious and immediate **shift** in attitude," says Laurie David, a producer of the movie *An Inconvenient Truth*, which helped to
50 raise awareness of the problem. Many believe that an attitude of hope and a desire to stay informed make a good beginning. As most would agree, an informed public is clearly in a better position to help address this critical issue.

---

2 An **outlet glacier** is a glacier that moves out from the edge of an ice sheet.

Overlooking the village of Ilulissat, the Jakobshavn glacier is slowly breaking apart, filling the ocean with huge pieces of ice.

Reading Comprehension

Multiple Choice. Choose the best answer for each question.

Gist

1. What is the main idea of this reading passage?
   a. Rising temperatures can cause global warming.
   b. Global warming is causing problems on Earth.
   c. Scientists are trying to slow the melting of glaciers.
   d. Global warming is melting ski areas all around the world.

Vocabulary

2. In line 7, the phrase *in the long run* means _____ .
   a. in the near future
   b. without stopping
   c. over a long period of time
   d. depending on the length of time

Vocabulary

3. In line 20, what does the quote *Reality is exceeding expectations* refer to?
   a. the Arctic ice melting faster than predicted
   b. people having no water to drink in Peru
   c. the sun getting hotter than scientists thought
   d. experts solving the global warming problem

Did You Know?

Sea ice provides habitats for many Arctic species. Due to the loss of ice, polar bears, the arctic fox, and four species of seals now face extinction.

Cause and Effect

4. What happens when water from melting ice gets between a glacier and the rock below?
   a. The water under the glacier freezes.
   b. The glacier slides forward more easily.
   c. The rocks absorb more heat from the sun.
   d. The glacier reflects more heat from the sun.

Detail

5. What do some researchers believe will happen by the year 2100?
   a. Global sea levels will rise by at least a meter.
   b. There will be no more ice in the Arctic Ocean.
   c. The ice sheet of Antarctica will have completely melted.
   d. There will be fewer heat waves and droughts all over the world.

Inference

6. Which of these statements would Laurie David probably agree with?
   a. Global warming is a problem that will fix itself over time.
   b. The average person can't do much to affect global warming.
   c. To stop global warming, people need to change how they think.
   d. Global warming will only be a problem many years in the future.

Main Idea

7. What would be the best heading for the final paragraph?
   a. An Inconvenient Truth
   b. Placing Blame
   c. An Informed Public
   d. Determining the Issues

Identifying Types of Supporting Details

When the author of a text makes a claim, read the text around the sentence. Pay attention to how the claim is supported. Supporting details give extra weight and credibility to any claim. Often a claim is made or supported using one of these techniques.

Common sense: *It's clear that . . .*   *Most people would agree . . .*

Examples or reasons: *For example, . . .*   *One reason for this is . . .*

Facts or statistics: **(general knowledge or historical)** *It's a fact that this happened . . .*
                           (measurements) *50% of the people . . .*

Expert opinion: *One expert claims . . .*   *According to a recent research study, . . .*

A. Multiple Choice. Look back at the reading on pages 147–149. Are these claims supported by: **(a)** common sense, **(b)** examples or reasons, **(c)** facts or statistics, or **(d)** expert opinion? Write **a**, **b**, **c**, or **d** for each statement below.

1. _____ Jakobshavn Isbræ glacier is moving toward the sea at a faster rate than expected. (paragraph 3)

2. _____ The glaciers of the Himalayas and the Andes could disappear in this century. (paragraph 5)

3. _____ An increasing number of heat waves and droughts worldwide suggests global warming is having an impact on humans right now. (paragraph 5)

4. _____ An informed public is in a better position to help address the issue of global warming. (paragraph 6)

∧ Tourists visit a waterfall formed by the melting ice of a glacier.

B. Analyzing. Circle any words in the passage that helped you determine the type of supporting detail the author used.

Critical Thinking Discuss with a partner. Has the climate changed recently where you live? In what way? What can individual people do about global warming? What can governments do?

Vocabulary Practice

A. Definitions. Read the information below. Then complete the definitions using the words in **red**.

In 2004, the movie *The Day After Tomorrow* gave people a look at some of global warming's **unexpected** effects. In the movie, polar ice melts, creating a variety of **critical** weather events. For example, Scotland freezes and New York is hit by giant waves. Most experts agree that the science of the movie was incorrect, but warn that as the ocean **absorbs** and continues to store heat, global warming could cause a huge **shift** in climate and perhaps even extreme weather. Since then, documentaries like *The 11th Hour* have given people a more accurate picture of the **consequences** of global warming and what can be done.

1. When a piece of cloth _____ water, it takes it in.

2. A(n) _____ situation is very serious and dangerous.

3. A(n) _____ occurs when something moves or changes position.

4. _____ are things that happen, usually negative, as a result of previous actions.

5. If something is _____, you did not think that it would happen.

B. Completion. Complete each sentence with a word from the box.

crack	exceed	host	slide	unstoppable

1. In 2018, Pyeongchang in South Korea will _____ the Winter Olympic Games.

2. Some holes in the ice are so big that lakes form in the middle of a glacier. A _____ in a glacier, which water enters, is called a *moulin*.

3. Once a disaster like an earthquake begins, it is _____. You just have to wait for it to end.

4. When the floor is wet and slippery, you can _____ across it.

5. If you _____ the speed limit while driving, you are breaking a law and should slow down.

> **Word Partnership**
> Use *host* with:
> (n.) host **country**, host **family**;
> (adj.) **charming** host;
> (v.) **act as** host, **play** host.

WALRUS HUNT

— Winter hunt route

▢ Variable ice thickness during winter

North Pole
Ellesmere I.

▢ AREA ENLARGED

CANADA

GREENLAND (Denmark)

ARCTIC CIRCLE

— Maximum extent of sea ice

Smith Sound

Siorapaluk

Qeqertarsuaq

Start and Finish
Qaanaaq (Thule)

Inglefield Fjord

Kiatak

Moriusaq

Baffin Bay

Appat

GREENLAND (Denmark)

THULE AIR BASE

0 mi ———— 25
0 km ———— 25

SOURCE: DIGITAL GLOBE, GOOGLE EARTH (SUMMER SATELLITE IMAGE)
NG MAPS

LAST DAYS OF
THE ICE HUNTERS

∧ The route taken by Inuit hunters during a walrus hunt. The Inuit are the native peoples of the Arctic. Until recently, many Inuit families have survived on only food found in the wild, but this is getting harder to do.

Before You Read

A. Discuss. Look at the map above and answer the questions.

1. Where does the hunt take place?

2. In which season does the hunt take place?

3. In which city does the hunt begin and end?

4. Why do you think the hunters want the walruses?

B. Predict. How do the hunters travel the route shown by the red lines on the map above? Check (✓) your guess. Then read the passage to check your ideas.

☐ by small airplane ☐ by boat

☐ by dogsled ☐ on skis

A Life on the Ice

Jens Danielsen kneels on his dogsled as it slides along the rough edge of a frozen sea. "*Harru, harru*," he calls out **urgently**. "Go left, go left. *Atsuk, atsuk*. Go right, go right." The 15 dogs in his team move carefully. Despite the freezing temperatures of the Arctic in late March, the ice is thin and has broken up, making travel dangerous. "The sea ice used to be three feet thick here," Danielsen says. "Now it's only four inches thick." Global warming is clearly having an unfavorable effect on the amount of sea ice needed for hunting.

As big as a bear and with a kind, boyish face, Danielsen is a 45-year-old ice hunter from Qaanaaq, a village of about 650 people whose brightly painted houses cover a hillside overlooking a fjord.[1] He's heading toward the ice edge to find walruses, as Inuit hunters have done for as long as they and their ancestors can remember. With his extended family and 57 dogs to feed, he will need to kill several walruses on this trip.

In the past, a thick shelf of ice would cover parts of the ocean near northwestern Greenland in September and stay until June. But for a number of years, the ice has been thick and the hunting good for only three or four weeks. The ice shelf gives hunters access to walruses, seals, and whales. Without the ice, hunting these creatures becomes nearly impossible. One winter, Qaanaaq's hunters found themselves without **sufficient** food to feed their **starving** dogs. The hunters, understandably, asked for help. The government responded with money, while fishing **corporations** assisted by sending in fish by airplane. And the hunters and their families survived one more year out on the ice.

---

1 A **fjord** is a narrow body of water cut into a valley by a glacier.

Where the ice is thin and melting, even sled-dogs are afraid to go. This hunter has to drag his dogs to move forward.

Sadly, today, fewer than 500 ice hunters are able to live by hunting alone. They travel by dogsled, wear skins, and hunt with harpoons,[2] just as their ancestors did. At the same time, they now also use guns and cell phones, and watch TV. "This changing weather is bad for us," Danielsen says, scowling.[3] "Some [of our] people have to go other ways to make **a living**." His wife, Ilaitsuk, who used to go with him on these hunting trips, has had to take a job at a day-care center in Qaanaaq to help pay their **bills**. The government now **funds** job training programs to help ice hunters find other employment.

Warmer weather does provide some opportunities. **Quantities** of valuable fish that prefer warmer water are increasing, and melting ice has uncovered some of Greenland's valuable natural **resources**—minerals, metals, and gems.[4] Electric power **plants**, with the promise of new jobs, may soon be built on rivers filled by melting ice. But the last ice hunters may not be able to get used to working as fishermen, in mines, or in power plants. As Danielsen says, "Without ice, we can't live. Without ice, we're nothing at all."

2 A **harpoon** is a long, pointed weapon with a rope attached to it, which is used to hunt large sea animals.

3 When someone **scowls**, an angry expression appears on his or her face.

4 A **gem** is a beautiful, usually shiny, stone used in jewelry.

Reading Comprehension

Multiple Choice. Choose the best answer for each question.

Gist

1. What is the passage mainly about?
   a. how to hunt sea animals in Greenland
   b. how the government is helping failed hunters
   c. how warmer weather is affecting Inuit hunters
   d. how modern hunting methods are better than traditional ones

Cause and Effect

2. Which of these is NOT an effect of Greenland's thinner ice?
   a. smaller fish and seals
   b. a shorter hunting season
   c. decreased access to food
   d. the hunters' need to find other jobs

Did You Know?

Nearly 50 percent of the rise in sea levels caused by global warming isn't because of melting ice. It's because water absorbs heat. As water gets warmer, it takes up more space.

Vocabulary

3. In line 30, which phrase could best replace the words *at the same time*?
   a. quickly   b. even though they do this
   c. during this time   d. on the other hand

Detail

4. What has made hunting with dogsleds difficult?
   a. The ice is too thin.
   b. There is too much ice.
   c. The dogs eat too much.
   d. There are not enough dogs.

Main Idea

5. What is the main idea of the fourth paragraph?
   a. The ice hunters have improved their hunting methods.
   b. Only the best ice hunters have been able to continue.
   c. More ice hunters have been able to improve their lives.
   d. The traditional ice hunters' way of life is disappearing.

Inference

6. Why might the ice hunters find it difficult to do other work?
   a. There is no training available.
   b. The government is unhelpful.
   c. They prefer their own traditions.
   d. There are few other jobs available.

Paraphrase

7. In line 45, what does Danielsen mean when he says, *without ice, we're nothing at all*?
   a. There will soon be no more ice.
   b. Our traditions depend on the ice.
   c. No hunter will ever do another job.
   d. Hunting on the ice is now too dangerous.

Identifying an Author's Tone or Point of View

The tone of a reading often expresses the feeling or attitude the author has toward a subject. An author may have a certain tone in one part of a text and a different tone in another part. To determine the tone, pay careful attention to your reaction as you read, and identify any words that make you react a certain way. Ask yourself if the word is positive or negative.

A. Classification. Categorize the words below to complete the chart. Is each word positive or negative?

artificial	brilliant	careless	childish	considerate	
encouraging	fortunate	irresponsible	jealous	stubborn	warm

Positive	Negative

B. Multiple Choice. The sentences below are from the passage on pages 154–155. Choose the words that best describe the author's tone. Then underline the word(s) that helped you answer the question.

1. Global warming is clearly having an unfavorable effect on the amount of sea ice needed for hunting. (paragraph 1)
   a. serious   b. confused   c. joyful   d. excited

2. The hunters, understandably, asked for help. (paragraph 3)
   a. joyful   b. pessimistic   c. sympathetic   d. angry

Critical Thinking Discuss with a partner.
Do you think the government and/or other organizations should help the ice hunters maintain their way of life? Why or why not? Are any traditional practices disappearing where you live? How do you feel about it?

An Inuit hunter dressed in furs

Vocabulary Practice

A. Completion. Complete the information with the words in the box.
One word is extra.

funds	quantity	starving	sufficient	urgent

During the summer, polar bears generally eat very little.
They instead rely on the large **1.** _____ of
fat in their bodies built up from last year's seal hunting.
At the end of a long summer without food, the polar
bears are **2.** _____. Their need for food is
sometimes so **3.** _____, they have been
known to kill and eat each other for food. Polar bears
can only hunt effectively when winter begins and there
is sea ice. Recent climate changes are shortening the icy
season. This means that the time the bears have to hunt
may no longer be **4.** _____ for their needs.

> ∧ At the end of the
> summer, polar bears
> can be very thin and
> weak. They will need
> to find food quickly
> to survive.

B. Words in Context. Complete each sentence with the
correct answer.

1. A **corporation** is a _____.

   a. new technology   b. business

2. When someone sends you a **bill**, they want you to _____.

   a. donate money   b. pay them for goods or services

3. Something that is **urgent** _____.

   a. is worth a lot of money   b. must be done very soon

4. If someone **funds** a program, he or she _____ it.

   a. works for   b. gives money to

5. A **resource** is something that can _____.

   a. help you succeed   b. stop you from succeeding

6. If you make **a living** from something, you use it to _____.

   a. improve your health   b. earn money

7. An electrical **plant** is a _____.

   a. tree that is struck by lightning   b. building where electricity is made

> **Usage**
> **I'm starving!** In
> informal English,
> people often say
> "I'm starving!" to
> mean that they
> are extremely
> hungry.

VIEWING Greenland's Melting Glaciers

Before You Watch

A. Predict. The pictures below show the size of the Greenland ice sheet. Look at the pictures and read the information. What could happen to Greenland's ice in the year 2100? Discuss with a partner.

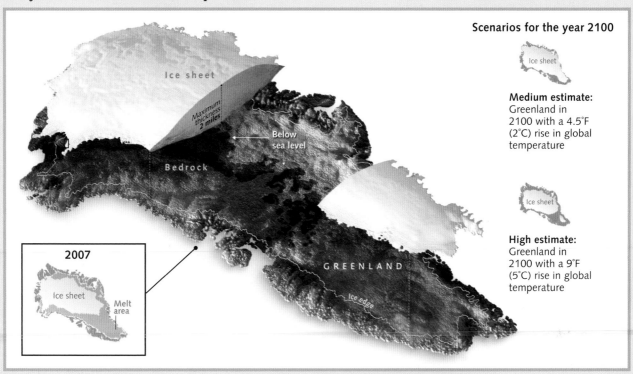

Scenarios for the year 2100

Medium estimate: Greenland in 2100 with a 4.5°F (2°C) rise in global temperature

High estimate: Greenland in 2100 with a 9°F (5°C) rise in global temperature

B. Completion. Complete the information with words from the box.

approaching	compressed	computer models	measures	rapidly

The Arctic ice sheet covers most of Greenland. It **1.** _____ more than 1.7 million square kilometers. Scientists once thought it was too big to melt. But recent temperatures have been **2.** _____ 26°C (a record high), and the ice is now melting **3.** _____. In some places, the melting has uncovered a layer of ice filled with bubbles. Scientists believe the bubbles were formed when air was **4.** _____ into the ice—squeezed into layers of ice—over time. Some bubbles are 400,000 years old. The scientists can put what they learn from these ancient gases into **5.** _____. These programs can show us what the environment was like then.

While You Watch

A. Sequencing. Read the statements below. Then as you watch, number them in the order they are mentioned. One statement is not mentioned.

_____ You can talk to the ice.

_____ There is one solution to the problem that most scientists agree on.

_____ The water gets under the glacier, causing it to slide slowly into the sea.

_____ Now, the ice is melting into the sea faster than at any time in history.

_____ The melting may result in sea levels rising three or four feet over the next century.

_____ Warming causes a faster loss of ice, and the loss of ice causes faster warming.

After You Watch

A. Completion. Complete the cause-and-effect diagram below with these events.

a. The ice sheet melts.
b. Water gets under the glacier.
c. The glacier's ice slides into the sea.
d. Sea levels rise. Warming seas absorb more heat.
e. Melted ice flows down holes in the glacier.

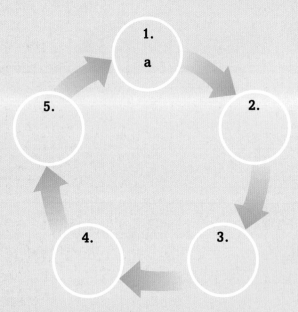

B. Discuss. Discuss these questions with a partner.

1. How important do you think it is to slow global warming? Are there any issues or global problems you feel are more important? Why?

2. In the video, the warming of the Arctic is described as a "vicious cycle." What does this mean?

3. Does global warming have any benefits? What countries or people might benefit from it?

11

INCREDIBLE INSECTS

A praying mantis carrying a flower. A mantis's arms are uniquely shaped for grabbing and holding its food.

Warm Up

Discuss these questions with a partner.

1. Are there any insects that you particularly like or dislike? Why?

2. Which insects do you think are the most beautiful?

3. What interesting facts do you know about insects?

Before You Read

A. Scan. What do you think army ants can do as a group? Read the paragraph below to find out.

Forget lions, tigers, and bears. When it comes to the art of war, army ants are among the most frightening creatures on Earth. With powerful mouth parts, these fighters are very skilled at cutting creatures much larger than themselves into pieces. Acting together in great numbers, army ant colonies[1] succeed at making tens of thousands of such kills each day. However, contrary to popular belief, they almost never take down large animals or people.

B. Predict. Choose the best answer for the question below. Then read the passage to check your answer.

Look at the photo and caption above. A *bivouac* is how the ants _____.

a. fight   b. eat
c. make nests   d. climb trees

⌃ Army ants use their own bodies to form "living bridges" (pictured above), and bivouacs, which they hang beneath a fallen tree.

1 An **ant colony** is a group of ants that live together in an organized society.

ARMY ANTS

A trail of army ants covers the forest floor.

1 　One of the best places to **observe** army ants is Barro Colorado, an island in a lake created by the Panama Canal. The island is home to as many as 50 colonies of *Eciton burchellii*, the most studied army ant in the world.

5 　The colonies of this army ant are huge, ranging from 300,000 to 700,000 ants. **Linking** their legs together, they have the capability to use their own bodies to form enormous **nests** called *bivouacs*. There they stay for about 20 days as the queen lays as many as 300,000 eggs. When the ants go

10 　hunting, as many as 200,000 of them leave the nest in a group that **broadens** into a fan as wide as 14 meters across. The *swarm raid* takes a slightly different course each day, allowing the hunters to cover fresh ground.

　Protecting the ants wherever they go are the soldiers,

15 　recognizable by their unusual, oversized jaws. The soldiers have a powerful bite—but their attack is almost always suicidal.[1] Because their jaws are shaped like fishhooks, it's impossible for the soldiers to pull them out again. Amazonian tribes have used soldier ants to close wounds, breaking off the

20 　bodies and leaving the heads in place.

　Eciton burchellii are blind and can't see what's ahead of them, but they move together in such great numbers that they easily kill the non-army ants, insects, and other small creatures that **constitute** their **prey**. When the group happens upon a break

25 　in the path, ants immediately link legs together and form a living bridge so that they can move forward without any **delay**.

　In Japanese, the word *ant* is written by linking two characters: one meaning "insect," the other meaning "**loyalty**." Indeed,

30 　individual ants are completely loyal to their **fellow** ants. They display many examples of selfless **cooperation** that, while certainly extreme, can't fail to win human admiration.

---

1 In a **suicidal** attack, the attacker loses its life in carrying out the attack.

Reading Comprehension

Multiple Choice. Choose the best answer for each question.

Detail
1. Barro Colorado is _____.
   a. the only place army ants live
   b. a good place to study army ants
   c. the most common type of army ant
   d. where army ants originally came from

Detail
2. As many as _____ army ants take part in a single swarm raid.
   a. 200,000   b. 300,000
   c. 700,000   d. a million

Detail
3. Which of the following statements about soldier ants is NOT true?
   a. They lay many eggs.
   b. They have a powerful bite.
   c. They can be used to close wounds.
   d. Their jaws are shaped like fishhooks.

Inference
4. Why does the author say the soldiers' attacks are suicidal?
   a. because the author thinks they are very strong
   b. because the Amazonians use them to close wounds
   c. because their jaws are shaped like fishhooks
   d. because they can't get away after they attack

Vocabulary
5. In line 24, the phrase *happens upon* is closest in meaning to _____.
   a. meets   b. avoids
   c. causes   d. needs

Paraphrase
6. What does the author mean by *form a living bridge* (lines 25–26)?
   a. make a bridge from plants
   b. walk across a man-made bridge
   c. make themselves into a bridge
   d. cover the path with insects they catch

Main Idea
7. The main idea of the final paragraph is that the author is impressed with _____.
   a. Japanese ants because of their loyalty
   b. the way the word *ant* is written in Japanese
   c. the way ants work well together as a team
   d. how language can describe ants so well

Did You Know?

Because army ants are blind, certain insects, like stick insects, have learned to escape their attacks by staying perfectly still.

Understanding Prefixes and Suffixes

Prefixes and suffixes are added to words in order to create new words with different meanings. Here are some common examples:

Prefixes	Examples	Suffixes	Examples
in-/im- (not)	*inactive*	**-al** (characteristic of)	*musical*
non- (not)	*nonfiction*	**-en** (become)	*lengthen*
over- (over, too much)	*overcook*	**-er** (one who)	*worker*
pre- (before)	*preview*	**-ful** (full of)	*fearful*
re- (again, back)	*replace*	**-less** (without)	*fearless*
un- (not)	*unfriendly*	**-ion/-tion** (act or process)	*attraction*

A. Definitions. In each sentence, underline the word that contains a prefix or suffix from the box above. Then write a short definition for the underlined word.

1. Weaver ants can create very complex leaf nests.
   Definition: _____

2. To make the nests, the ants form chains with their bodies, then shorten the chain one ant at a time.
   Definition: _____

3. The silk used to glue the leaf edges is produced by immature ants.
   Definition: _____

4. All the ants cooperate to carry out the nest construction together.
   Definition: _____

5. Scientists think we could invent some antlike robots to perform useful tasks.
   Definition: _____

B. Scan. Look back at the reading on page 163. Find and write a word that contains each prefix or suffix.

1. *-ers* (paragraph 2) _____
2. *un-* (paragraph 3) _____
3. *over-* (paragraph 3) _____
4. *non-* (paragraph 4) _____
5. *-less* (paragraph 5) _____

Critical Thinking Discuss with a partner. The reading passage describes ants as "loyal." What other animals can be described as loyal? Give reasons for your opinion.

Vocabulary Practice

A. Completion. Complete the information below using the words in the box.

constitute	fellow	loyalty	nests	observed	prey

Argentine ant **1.** _____ have been discovered across Italy, France, Spain, and Portugal. Taken together, they **2.** _____ a "supercolony" 6,000 kilometers long. Scientists have **3.** _____ that ants from this supercolony never fight with their **4.** _____ ants. Unfortunately, Argentine ants seem to feel no **5.** _____ toward ants from other species. They kill and eat them as they would any other **6.** _____.

B. Words in Context. Complete each sentence with the correct answer.

1. When you **link** two or more things, you _____.
   a. identify their differences   b. connect them to each other

2. If you **broaden** a road or path, you make it _____.
   a. wider   b. narrower

3. You _____ trust a person who is **loyal** to you.
   a. can   b. cannot

4. When insects **cooperate**, they _____.
   a. work together   b. fight each other

5. A traffic **delay** could cause you to get home _____ than planned.
   a. earlier   b. later

< More than 10,000 known ant species are found around the world. They typically eat nectar, seeds, fungus, or other insects.

> **Word Link**
> The prefix **co-** is used to form verbs or nouns that refer to people sharing things or doing things together, e.g., *cooperate, coexist, co-produce, co-worker, co-owner.*

1

2

3

UNEXPECTED
BEAUTY

Before You Read

A. Discuss. Look at the photos above, and read the information below.

1. The photos above show **a)** a butterfly, **b)** a moth, and **c)** a dragonfly. Label the pictures with the insects' names.

2. How would you describe each insect? Think about its colors, patterns, and shape.

> Can you tell these insects apart? Although they are similar in some ways, there are also many differences between them. For example, moths usually rest with their wings spread out flat. Butterflies often fold their wings behind their backs. Moths have rough, hairy bodies, while the bodies of butterflies are smoother. Butterflies have bright colors on their wings. Most (but not all) moths have a dull appearance. The third creature, a dragonfly, belongs to a completely different insect family. They have long, thin bodies and strong, transparent wings.

B. Skimming for the Main Idea. Skim the reading on pages 168–169. What is the reading passage mainly about?

a. how paintings of moths made an important contribution to science

b. how moths were caught and images produced for an interesting display

c. how scientists are photographing moths with very low populations

The Beauty of Moths

For many people, moths are swarming, dust-colored pests that eat our clothes and disturb us by flying around lights after dark. However, to artist Joseph Scheer, they are creatures of beauty. The images he creates bring out the beauty of moths, with colors, shapes, and patterns that have never before been seen so clearly. "**Digital** tools let you see things you'd never see just looking with your eyes," Scheer says. Scheer's images have been displayed around the world, and one **reaction** is heard everywhere: "People insist, 'No, that can't be a moth,'" says Scheer. One Swiss viewer **credited** the insects' lovely variety to their **exotic** American origin: "We don't have such nice moths in our country," he **declared**. In fact, every country has moths that can amaze.

The process began with a moth hunt in the state of New York. Scheer would leave the lights on and windows open overnight at his university office. He later returned to collect the moths that had flown in. When the building cleaners **complained**, he moved the hunt to his friend Mark Klingensmith's yard. "Mark's a gardener with lots of stuff growing on his property," Scheer says. "Moths like it." They set up lights shining over a plastic container on a white sheet. Then they watched as moths **emerged** from the darkness, flew carelessly into the sheet, and fell into the plastic container. "We got a different species every night that first season," Scheer says. "The patterns and colors were **overwhelming**."

Scanning the Details

Using a powerful scanner[1] designed for camera film, they were able to capture detailed pictures of moths. Small moths present special challenges. "One twitch of the finger and there goes a wing," says Scheer. "I try to drink less coffee when I'm working on [them]."

The scanner records so much information that a single moth can take 20 minutes to scan. A scan of just two small moths fills an entire CD. All that information means the size of an image can be increased 2,700 percent but still **retain** all the details and appear perfectly clear. You'd need a microscope[2] to see the details shown in Scheer's prints.

Scheer's work is not only a new form of art. He can also be **congratulated** for making a valuable contribution to the record of moths where he lives. He has helped identify more than a thousand different species. "Not from Alaska or the Amazon," Klingensmith says. "All from one backyard."

> The delicate coloring of a moth's wing

---

1 A **scanner** is a machine that can take pictures for use on computers.
2 A **microscope** is a scientific tool that allows small objects to appear larger, so that details can be seen.

Over 20 species of moth cover a wall in Scheer's studio. His photographs have been shown in countries around the world.

Reading Comprehension

Multiple Choice. Choose the best answer for each question.

Inference
1. People think, "No, that can't be a moth" because _____.
   a. they know the images are not really of moths
   b. the images look like they are only paintings
   c. the images seem too beautiful to be moths
   d. most countries don't have such beautiful moths

Detail
2. The moth hunt moved from Scheer's office to Klingensmith's yard because _____.
   a. there were no moths at the university
   b. the cost of electricity was too high
   c. they began to catch the same types of moths
   d. the building cleaners were complaining

Inference
3. What does Scheer mean when he says, "One twitch of the finger and there goes a wing"?
   a. His fingers often twitch when he's working.
   b. He usually takes the wings off the moths first.
   c. He has to work very fast to capture the images.
   d. He has to be very careful working with the moths.

Fact or Opinion
4. Which of the following quotes is not a fact, but a person's opinion?
   a. "Moths like it."
   b. "Mark's a gardener with lots of stuff growing on his property."
   c. "We got a different species every night that first season."
   d. "I try to drink less coffee when I'm working on [them]."

Detail
5. The images retain all the details even when increased 2,700 percent because _____.
   a. a microscope is used to prepare the images
   b. very high quality paint is used to create the images
   c. the moths have very bright colors and clear patterns
   d. the scanner records a lot of information for each picture

Vocabulary
6. In line 35, the phrase *not only* is closest in meaning to _____.
   a. more than just
   b. nonetheless
   c. not at all
   d. in addition

Inference
7. Why does Klingensmith mention Alaska and the Amazon?
   a. because he hopes to go to those places in the future
   b. because we might expect to see amazing moths there
   c. because moths there are very different from those in his yard
   d. because he has helped identify more than a thousand species there

Did You Know?

The largest moth in the world is the Atlas moth of Southeast Asia. It can be 30 centimeters across in length.

Reading Skill

Summarizing a Text

A *summary* is a short version of a longer text. Summarizing is a useful skill because it shows that you understand the main points of a text and can put them into your own words. These tips can help you as you prepare to create a summary:

- Read the text several times to be sure you understand it.
- Highlight, outline, and make notes about the most important information.
- State the main idea in the form of a thesis statement in the first line.
- Keep your summary short, concise, and in your own words.
- Include only information from the text. Avoid adding your own opinion to the summary.

A. Multiple Choice. Complete the thesis statement. Choose the main idea of the passage on pages 168–169.

Joseph Scheer and Mark Klingensmith _____.

a. have created a new form of art

b. enjoy painting moths in bright colors

c. show that moths and butterflies are similar species

d. prove that the prettiest moths come from the United States

B. Completion. Write the completed thesis statement from **A** on the first line below. Then complete the summary using **one word** from the reading for each blank.

Joseph Scheer and Mark Klingensmith _____
_____. They create images that truly bring out the

1. _____ of moths. The wonderful prints they make

are **2.** _____ all around the world. The two men

collect moths which are attracted to **3.** _____ that

they set up in Klingensmith's yard. They then use a

4. _____ to record extremely detailed images of

the moths. In addition, the pair has done valuable scientific work by

identifying more than 1,000 **5.** _____ of moth.

Critical Thinking Discuss with a partner. What other creatures do you think would be considered beautiful if we could look at them in a different way? Why?

∧ A long-tailed yellow moon moth

Vocabulary Practice

A. Completion. Complete the information with the words in the box. One word is extra.

declare	emerge	exotic	reaction	retain

Moths and their caterpillars are a favorite food of many animals, but nature has provided them with some defenses. Some **1.** _____ moth caterpillars feed on deadly plants. They **2.** _____ the deadly materials in their bodies, which make animals that eat them sick. When other caterpillars or moths are hunted by birds or other enemies, their **3.** _____ is to expose large spots on their skin that look like eyes, to frighten the enemy away. Most moths also only **4.** _____ at night, making it difficult for their enemies to see them.

B. Words in Context. Complete each sentence with the correct answer.

1. A **digital** system records information using _____.
   a. pen and paper   b. a computer

2. A scientist would be **congratulated** for making _____.
   a. a new discovery   b. a big mistake

3. An army that is **overwhelmed** probably_____.
   a. has an advantage   b. loses quickly

4. If you are **credited** with doing something, you are _____.
   a. believed to have done it   b. owed money for doing it

5. Someone who **declares** something probably _____.
   a. believes it strongly   b. isn't sure about it

6. When you **complain** about something, you _____ it.
   a. say bad things about   b. do something to change

A caterpillar displays its fake eyes.

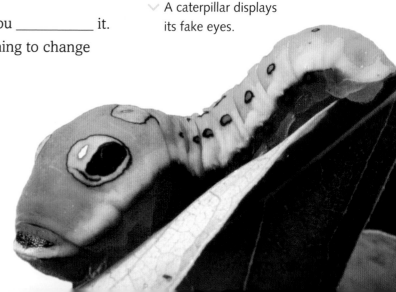

> **Word Partnership**
> Use *reaction* with: (*v.*) **get a** reaction; **provoke a** reaction; (*adj.*) **slow/quick** reaction, **delayed** reaction, **mixed** reaction.

VIEWING Kenya Butterflies

Before You Watch

A. Warm Up. Look at the four stages in the development of a butterfly. Which happens first? Number the pictures (1–4).

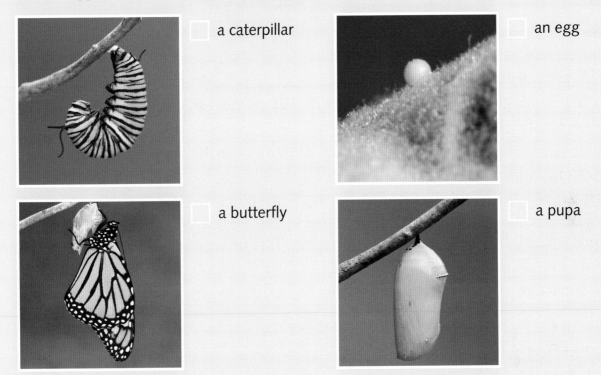

☐ a caterpillar

☐ an egg

☐ a butterfly

☐ a pupa

B. Discuss. In which of the stages do you think it would be best to send a butterfly to another country? Why?

While You Watch

A. Completion. Read the summary below. As you watch, complete the summary with information from the video.

Kenya has **1.** _____ species of butterflies. In the past, people caught live butterflies from **2.** _____ and sent them to collectors overseas. Now, local farmers have a different way to make money—rearing caterpillars to sell. The insects now have a 100 percent **3.** _____ rate. The project helps the local people see the **4.** _____ of conserving the forest. They can derive **5.** _____ from the forest. In a year, the farmers sell **6.** _____ U.S. dollars' worth of butterflies. The project now has over **7.** _____ workers.

After You Watch

A. Multiple Choice. Choose the best answer for each question below.

1. In the past, what was the problem with sending butterflies to other countries?

   a. Most butterflies were caught illegally.

   b. Many butterflies died before reaching their destination.

   c. People in other countries did not want these butterflies.

2. Which of the following are now being sent around the world?

   a. butterfly eggs

   b. caterpillar pupae

   c. live caterpillars

3. According to Washington Iemba, what's the main threat to East Africa's forests?

   a. diseases that kill important plants

   b. the increase in butterfly farms

   c. the cutting down of trees

4. What was the main objective for creating the Butterfly Farm Project?

   a. to develop support for the conservation of the forest

   b. to create an international market for Kenya's butterflies

   c. to increase the price of butterflies so farmers get a better income

5. According to Washington Iemba, what is the most attractive aspect of the project?

   a. It has helped save several butterfly species.

   b. The farmers are able to make money quickly.

   c. People can spend time with the butterflies.

B. Discuss. Discuss these questions with a partner.

1. Who do you think buys the butterflies? Why?

2. Would you like to buy a butterfly from the project? Why or why not?

3. What other insects do you think could be commercially traded?

In a butterfly farm, butterflies are fed sweet fruit. >

12

GOING TO EXTREMES

A caver climbs through a wet passage in McBride's Cave in Alabama, in the U.S.

Warm Up

Discuss these questions with a partner.

1. Do you admire adventurous people? Why or why not?

2. Where are the most extreme places a person might visit?

3. What are some of the most adventurous activities and sports you know? Which ones would you like to try?

1. The first successful _____ flight took place in 1903, when Wilbur and Orville Wright flew the *Wright Flyer* for 12 seconds.

2. _____ is the sport of jumping out of a plane. Once in the air, a person falls for about a minute before opening their parachute.

3. _____ is a lot like skydiving, but instead of airplanes, jumpers leap off places much closer to the ground. The letters B.A.S.E. stand for Building, Antenna (radio towers), Span (bridges), and Earth (cliffs).

Before You Read

A. Completion. Look at the pictures and captions on this and the next page. Complete the captions (1–4) with the words in the box.

airplane	BASE jumping	hang glider	skydiving

B. Discuss. Look at the photos and read the captions again. Then answer the questions with a partner.

1. Why do you think people enjoy sports like hang gliding?

2. Do you think "sky sports" are worth the risk? Why or why not?

C. Scan. What kind of flight does the author experience for the first time? Scan the passage and choose the correct answer.

a. flying in a plane   b. skydiving

c. BASE jumping   d. hang gliding

4. To fly with a _____, a person must run down a hill, letting air flow over the wing, lifting it into the air like a large kite.

THE DREAM OF FLIGHT

By Nancy Shute

1   For thousands of years, humans have dreamed of flying. The ancient Greeks told the legend of Icarus, a boy who flies so high that the sun melts his man-made wings and he comes crashing down to Earth. Across history, many more people
5   have died after jumping from a tower or **cliff** with man-made wings that didn't quite work. Flying, for humans, seemed an impossible **feat**.

Yet, many continued to dream of flying as free as birds. One such dreamer was the great 15th-century artist and inventor
10   Leonardo da Vinci. He studied the flight of birds and even designed his own flying machines, but they—and he—never left the ground.

Five hundred years later, standing on a windy hill in North Carolina, in the U.S., I was about to make the dream come true.

There are on average 22 sky-sport-related deaths recorded each year in the U.S. alone. Yet, despite the risks, sports involving human flight are becoming more popular, as many look to experience flight in a personal way.

15 Unlike Leonardo, I had the help of a hang glider—a light, modern machine that makes flying simple and safe enough even for tourist entertainment. I held on to the hang glider as **tightly** as I could. Terrified, I ran down the

20 hill. Suddenly, I was running in the air. I was flying! What a **thrill**! Now I wanted more.

A friend in my hang gliding class suggested I next try a "tandem flight." She explained that it's flying in a hang glider for two people.

25 A small airplane **tows** you up 600 meters into the air and lets you go. I decided to try it with my instructor, Jon Thompson. Up we went. When the airplane released us, it felt like falling from a building, headfirst. "You can fly

30 now," Jon said. After a few moments, I found the **courage** to turn the glider a little to the left, and then a little to the right. I was more like a pigeon[1] than an eagle,[2] but I was flying!

A model of a flying machine designed by Leonardo da Vinci

Of course, hang gliding is not the only way mankind has

35 learned to enjoy the freedom of flight. Today, some people skydive, while others—known as BASE jumpers—enjoy the excitement of jumping off buildings, cliffs, and bridges, often illegally. They free-fall[3] for a few exciting moments, and then open a parachute before hitting the ground. "It's as close as

40 human beings can get to flying like a bird," says BASE jumper J. T. Holmes.

Switzerland's Yves Rossy might disagree. The wings he has invented for personal flight have four small **engines**. He **steers** them just by moving his shoulders. For ten minutes

45 at a time, Rossy does seem to fly as free as a bird, having both power and control. One of his longest flights was across the water from France to England. "It's awesome, it's great, it's **fantastic**!" says Rossy. Since then, he has continued to improve his wing design, and hopes he can "**motivate** the

50 next generation of thinkers to do something different . . . even if it seems impossible."

1 A **pigeon** is a fat bird that usually lives in towns and cities.

2 An **eagle** is a large bird known for its strength, vision, and power of flight.

3 When skydivers **free-fall**, they fall downwards without anything to stop or slow them down.

Pilot and inventor Yves Rossy jumps from a plane wearing his jet engine-powered flight system. The two-meter-long wings allow Rossy to fly through the air at an average of 200 kilometers an hour.

Reading Comprehension

Multiple Choice. Choose the best answer for each question.

Gist

1. What is the first paragraph mainly about?
   a. Leonardo da Vinci's dream of flying
   b. why some people continue to try to fly
   c. how the Greeks were the first to try to fly
   d. how people have always dreamed of flying

Detail

2. How does the author describe her first hang gliding experience?
   a. interesting   b. terrible
   c. exciting   d. dangerous

Detail

3. What is true about a "tandem flight"?
   a. You control a small airplane.
   b. You are able to fly above 700 meters.
   c. You fly together with another person.
   d. You take off from the top of a building.

Vocabulary

4. What can the words *lets you go* in line 26 be replaced with?
   a. allows you   b. releases you
   c. connects you   d. guides you

Detail

5. What is NOT true about BASE jumping?
   a. Parachutes are used.
   b. People land on the ground.
   c. People jump from airplanes.
   d. BASE jumps are often illegal.

Reference

6. What does the word *it's* refer to in line 47?
   a. free-falling
   b. flying like a bird
   c. opening a parachute
   d. doing something illegal

Detail

7. What did Yves Rossy accomplish?
   a. He BASE jumped many times.
   b. He invented flying without wings.
   c. He invented wings that have engines.
   d. He flew a plane from France to England.

Did You Know?

The record for the highest BASE jump belongs to Russia's Valery Rozov. In 2013, he jumped off Mount Everest from a height of 7,220 meters (23,688 feet).

Reading Skill

Recognizing Similes

A *simile* is a figure of speech in which two unlike things are compared using *as* or *like*. Writers use similes to explain things, to express emotion, and to make their writing more entertaining to the reader. They are common in literature, but can appear in any kind of text. Here are some examples:

He's as blind as a bat.   *She ran like the wind.*
His hair was as black as coal.   *She has a temper like a volcano.*

A. Completion. Look back at the passage on pages 177–179. What are these experiences (1–3) compared to in the passage?

1. being released from an airplane _____

2. the way the author flew the hang glider _____

3. Rossy's experience of flying _____

B. Matching. The phrase **as + adjective + as + noun** is very common in English. Match the words and phrases to complete some similes.

1. as light as   •   • a. ice
2. as cold as   •   • b. silk
3. as busy as   •   • c. nails
4. as tough as   •   • d. a bee
5. as gentle as   •   • e. a lamb
6. as smooth as   •   • f. a feather

∧ A pigeon

C. Completion. Complete the similes below (1–4) with the words in the box.

| a bird   cats and dogs   a dog   a pig |

1. The couple is fighting like _____.

2. He makes a big mess when he eats. He eats like _____.

3. I'm so tired. All day, I've been working like _____.

4. Is that all you're going to eat? You eat like _____.

Critical Thinking Discuss with a partner. Which way of flying do you think is the safest? the most dangerous? the most exciting?

Vocabulary Practice

A. Completion. Complete the information below using the words in the box. Two words are extra.

courage	fantastic	feat	steered	thrill	tight	towed

Felix Baumgartner, skydiver, BASE jumper, and overall
1. _____ seeker, is now also known as the man
who fell from space.

▲ Felix Baumgartner
prepares to jump
from space.

"I'm coming home," he said, on October 14, 2012, just
before stepping out of a capsule **2.** _____ by a balloon
39 kilometers off the ground, into space.

After a four-minute, 22-second free-fall, the Austrian
skydiver opened his parachute and **3.** _____ it
to a safe landing spot. In total, he had spent ten minutes
in the air. In a later interview, Baumgartner admitted he
was terrified during the fall. But most would agree that in
accomplishing this amazing **4.** _____, "Fearless Felix"
has inspired the millions of people watching over the Internet,
and that he showed a level of **5.** _____ that few have.

B. Words in Context. Complete each sentence with the correct answer.

1. If you hold on to something **tightly**, it would be _____ to take
   it from you.
   a. easy   b. difficult

2. If someone falls off a **cliff**, they are likely falling off _____.
   a. a building   b. a mountain

3. When someone **tows** a car, they _____ it.
   a. push   b. pull

4. The **engine** of a _____ is what makes it move.
   a. bicycle   b. car

5. If something is described as **fantastic**, it is likely to be _____.
   a. really fun   b. really scary

6. When you **motivate** someone, you _____ something.
   a. stop them from doing   b. inspire them to do

> **Word Partnership**
> Use **thrill** with: (n.)
> thrill **seeker/ride/**
> **factor**; (adj.) **big/**
> **great/cheap** thrill.

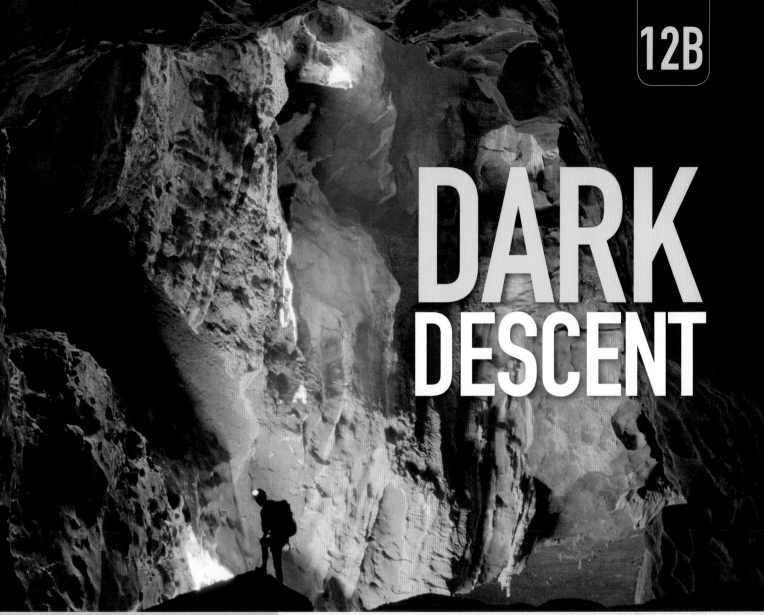

DARK
DESCENT

Making a **descent** into a **cave** system, explorers never know what they might find. As they move down long **passages**, light from the cave **entrance** soon disappears. In the blackness, they may come face-to-face with injury or death, or a discovery like none the world has ever seen.

Before You Read

A. Matching. Read the caption. Then match the correct form of each word in **bold** with its definition.

1. A(n) _____ is a movement from a higher to a lower level.

2. A(n) _____ is a (usually long) space that connects one place with another.

3. A(n) _____ is a way into a place, such as a door or an opening.

4. A(n) _____ is a large hole in the side of a cliff or hill, or under the ground.

B. Scan. Look at pages 184–185. What name did the cavers give to the deepest point of the cave they reached in 2004?

   a. Way to the Dream   b. Game Over   c. Millennium Pit

A caver is carefully lowered down on a rope. Above him is the entrance of Krubera Cave.

The Deepest Cave

It's August 2004. Caver Sergio García-Dils de la Vega kisses his girlfriend good-bye at the entrance of Krubera Cave. He doesn't know it yet, but Krubera, in the western Caucasus Mountains,[1] is the deepest known cave in the world. It will be weeks before he sees her again.

A member of an international team of 56 cavers from seven countries, García-Dils' mission was to explore Krubera. The team also hoped to be the first to reach a **depth** of 2,000 meters (6,562 feet), a feat compared to **conquering** the North and South Poles. One team member even describes descending into Krubera as "like climbing an inverted[2] Mount Everest."

Like climbers making their way up that famous peak, the cavers descend slowly. They climbed down ropes through huge tunnels, and crawled through tight passages. Bringing over five tons[3] of equipment and other **necessities** with them, they established underground camps along the route. At each camp, they stopped to rest, eat, sleep, and plan the next part of the journey. Some days, they worked for up to 20 hours at a time. And each day, they left miles of rope behind them to **ease** their return **ascent**, and telephone lines to communicate with people above.

1 The **Caucasus Mountains** are in the country of Georgia, between the Black Sea and the Caspian Sea.

2 Something that is **inverted** is upside down.

3 A **ton** is a unit of weight equal to 2,000 pounds or 909 kilograms.

In the third week, they reached 1,775 meters, the deepest point achieved by cavers so far. Here, progress was **blocked** by a sump—a passage filled with water. The cavers had only a few options: They could empty out all the water, dive through, or go around it. Gennady Samokhin dove to the bottom but was **disappointed**: "No chance to get through," he said. Searching for a way around the sump, García-Dils risked entering a cascade[4] of near freezing water. "The water was so cold, I lost the feeling in my fingers," he said. He, too, was unsuccessful.

Finally, the team found a way around the sump through a tight passage they called the "Way to the Dream." At first, they were **exhilarated**. However, it soon led to yet another sump at 1,840 meters. After a short test dive, Samokhin emerged, smiling. There was a promising passage, he reported. Sadly, it would have to wait. After nearly four weeks underground, with supplies running low, the team was **out of time**. They would have to return to the surface.

Four weeks later, following the path opened by García-Dils' team, a team of Ukrainian cavers reached the sump at 1,840 meters **relatively** quickly. After much searching, a pit[5] (named the "Millennium Pit") was discovered that allowed them to pass the 2,000-meter depth. More pits and passages led them to 2,080 meters, a spot they named "Game Over." But the caving game is never over. In 2009, Gennady Samokhin returned to Krubera. This time, he reached a depth of 2,191 meters. Then in 2012, he broke his own record, diving to a point six meters deeper, at a total depth of 2,197 meters. And so the caving game goes on, with deeper and deeper caves calling out to be explored.

---

4 A **cascade** is falling water.

5 In caving, a **pit** is part of a cave that falls straight down.

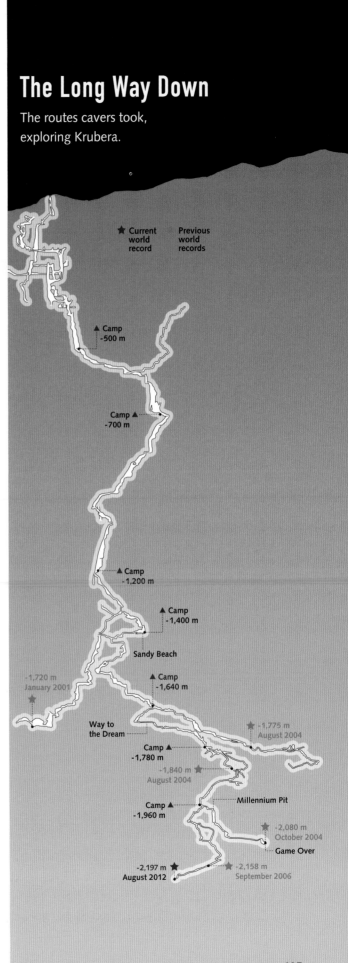

The Long Way Down

The routes cavers took, exploring Krubera.

★ Current world record   Previous world records

▲ Camp -500 m

Camp ▲ -700 m

▲ Camp -1,200 m

▲ Camp -1,400 m

Sandy Beach

-1,720 m January 2001

▲ Camp -1,640 m

Way to the Dream

★ -1,775 m August 2004

Camp ▲ -1,780 m

-1,840 m ★ August 2004

Millennium Pit

Camp ▲ -1,960 m

★ -2,080 m October 2004

Game Over

-2,197 m ★ August 2012

★ -2,158 m September 2006

Reading Comprehension

Multiple Choice. Choose the best answer for each question.

Gist

1. What is this passage mainly about?
   a. a cave near Mount Everest
   b. a journey of cave exploration
   c. equipment needed for caving
   d. famous caves around the world

Detail

2. Which of the following did García-Dils NOT bring into the cave?
   a. his girlfriend   b. food and water
   c. maps and ropes   d. telephone lines

Detail

3. How did the cavers solve the problem of the sump at 1,775 meters?
   a. They emptied it.
   b. They dove through it.
   c. They found a way around it.
   d. They weren't able to solve it.

Reference

4. The word *it* in line 38 refers to _____.
   a. the team   b. the sump
   c. the record   d. the passage

Inference

5. Why was Samokhin smiling as he emerged from a test dive?
   a. He had discovered another sump.
   b. He had found a new way to bring in supplies.
   c. He had possibly found a way through the sump.
   d. He was happy that he was returning to the surface.

Detail

6. About how deep did Samokhin descend in 2012?
   a. 1,775 meters   b. 2,080 meters
   c. 1,840 meters   d. 2,197 meters

Main Idea

7. What is the main idea of the last paragraph?
   a. to explain how a Ukrainian team rescued García-Dils' team
   b. to give reasons why another team followed a different path
   c. to describe how another team reached a depth of over 2,000 meters
   d. to illustrate the thrill the team felt when they finished their descent

Did You Know?

Some caves, like this one, are underwater. Some have underwater tunnels that go on for many kilometers. In 2007, Jarrod Jablonski and Casey McKinlay dove through a tunnel in Florida that took them six hours to reach the end of.

Synthesizing Information from Multiple Sources

When you read a passage, it's important to read all the information related to the text. This can include footnotes, photo captions, charts, graphs, timelines, and maps. They can contain important information that, at times, you may need to combine with information from the text to fully comprehend the passage.

A. Analyzing. Look back at pages 184–185. Check (✓) which things are included with the reading text.

- ☐ a footnote
- ☐ a map
- ☐ a chart
- ☐ a graph
- ☐ a photo
- ☐ a caption

B. Multiple Choice. Look back at pages 184–185 again. Then choose the correct answer for each question.

1. In what country is the Krubera Cave?

   a. Georgia   b. Russia   c. Ukraine   d. Turkey

2. Who or what is mentioned both in a photo caption and in the passage?

   a. Samokhin   b. the entrance of Krubera Cave
   c. García-Dils   d. the "Millennium Pit"

3. What is shown on the map but NOT mentioned in the passage?

   a. underground camps   b. earlier expedition routes
   c. a cascade   d. the "Way to the Dream"

4. How many people in total were there in García-Dils' team?

   a. 4   b. 6   c. 20   d. 56

Critical Thinking Discuss with a partner. What can we learn from exploring caves? Can we apply what is learned elsewhere? Do you think caves like Krubera should be open to tourists? Why or why not?

∧ Caver Sergio García-Dils de la Vega kisses his girlfriend good-bye at the entrance of Krubera Cave.

Vocabulary Practice

A. Definitions. Use the correct form of the words in the box to complete the definitions below. There are two extra words.

ascend	block	conquer	depth	disappoint
ease	exhilarated	necessity	out of time	relatively

1. Something that _____ your way stops you from moving forward.
2. A(n) _____ is something that you must have.
3. If you are _____ , you feel happy and excited.
4. When you _____ something, you overcome the challenges it presents; or you take control of it.
5. In an exam, when the bell rings and you haven't finished your test, you are _____ .
6. If you _____ something, you make it less difficult to do.
7. When you _____ a mountain, you move upwards to the peak.
8. Someone who is _____ healthy is healthy compared to unhealthy people.

B. Completion. Complete the information below with the correct form of the words in **A**. Four words are extra.

At the invitation of the government, cave expert Louise Hose had come to view the caves of Oman. Her goal was to see if they could be made **1.** _____ safe; safe enough for tourists, increasing Oman's options for new tourist attractions. At the Well of Birds, a very beautiful green pit with a(n) **2.** _____ of 210 meters, Hose used climbing ropes to **3.** _____ her way down.

Above her, two local men watched, fascinated by the female caver. They had never seen a woman so familiar with caving techniques. Soon, Hose joined her group at the bottom of the pit, where they were **4.** _____ to discover that a black pool was **5.** _____ their way to the cave entrance. They swam to the other side, where they saw the water spill out of the pool and disappear into the cave system. There, they stopped to rest, feeling **6.** _____ by the natural beauty around them and the incredible feat they had accomplished.

∧ Louise Hose lowers herself into Tawi Attair, the Well of Birds.

Word Partnership
Use **necessity** with: (adj.)
absolute necessity,
economic necessity,
political necessity.

VIEWING Sky Shooter

Before You Watch

Traveling at speeds of 160 kilometers an hour, over 4 km above the ground, these 71 skydivers broke a world record for skydiving in wing suits.

A. Warm Up. Look at the photo. Then discuss the questions below with a partner.

1. What part of the skydiving experience do you think would be the most terrifying? the most exciting? the most dangerous?
2. How do you think the photographer took this picture?
3. What qualities would a sky shooter (someone who photographs skydivers in the air) need to have?

While You Watch

A. True or False. Read the sentences below. Then, as you watch the video, mark them as true (**T**) or false (**F**).

1. Sanders has several minutes to film a free fall from a helicopter.   **T**   **F**
2. Sanders films a man jumping out of a jet plane.   **T**   **F**
3. Sanders and Paul Waschak are connected when they jump.   **T**   **F**
4. Sanders will probably go skydiving again.   **T**   **F**

After You Watch

A. Matching. Check (✓) the caption that best describes each picture from the video.

1. ☐ There are 5,000 skydivers at the convention.
☐ At the convention, the skydivers will make 500 jumps.

2. ☐ Sanders films skydivers from inside a helicopter.
☐ Sanders films while skydiving from a helicopter.

3. ☐ Paul Waschak is ready to "jump the jet."
☐ Paul Waschak is ready to "film the feat."

4. ☐ Sanders makes a picture-perfect landing.
☐ Sanders makes a less than perfect landing.

B. Discuss. Read what Tom Sanders said about capturing the experience of free-falling. Then discuss the questions below with a partner.

> "I don't think it's possible to capture on film what it's like to be in a free fall. I think you can capture some incredible images and you can get people's imaginations inspired, but I don't think unless you do it, you can appreciate the beauty and the thrill and the freedom of flying through the air."

1. What does Sanders mean by his statement? Do you think he's right?

2. What other things do you think can only be truly appreciated by experiencing them firsthand?

Photo Credits

1 Frans Lanting/NGC, **3, 176** (tr) Oliver Furrer/Stockbyte/Getty Images, **4–5, 86–87** (c), **88–90** (t) Georgette Douwma/Getty Images, **7** Jim Richardson/NGC, **8** (tr) mlisager/E+/Getty Images, **8** (cr) Hong Vo/Shutterstock, **8** (br) Elena Schweitzer/Shutterstock, **8** (tl) Ruth Black/Shutterstock, **8** (bl) M. Unal Ozmen/Shutterstock, **9** (r) Ruth Black/Shutterstock, **10–12** (t) Luciano Mortula/Shutterstock, **10** (br) Juris Sturainis/Shutterstock, **11** (tr) Maks Narodenko/Shutterstock, **12** (br) Maynard Owen Williams/NGC, **13** (cl), **13** (tc), **13** (tl), **13** (tr), **13** (bl) Jim Richardson/NGC, **13** (br) Ian 2010/Shutterstock, **14** (tr) Jim Richardson/NGC, **14–15** (b), **16–18** (t) GardenPhotos.com/Alamy, **16** (cr), **17** (cr), **18** (cr) Jim Richardson/NGC, **20** (tl) Christian Jung/Shutterstock, **20** (tr) Deyan Georgiev/Shutterstock, **20** (cl) Martin M303/Shutterstock, **20** (cr) Flower Power/Shutterstock, **21** Michael Nichols/NGC, **22–23** Eduardo Lugo/National Geographic My Shot/NGC, **24–25, 26–28** (t) Richard Robinson/Cultura Limited/SuperStock, **26** (br) Monica & Michael Sweet/Perspectives/Getty Images, **29** Carl Lyttle/Stone/Getty Images, **30** (t) Bernard Weil/Toronto Star/Getty Images, **31** (br) Marion Fichter/age fotostock, **31** (tr) Susan Schmitz/Shutterstock, **32, 34** (t) Erik Lam/Shutterstock, **32** (br) Sovfoto/UIG/Getty Images, **33** (t) cynoclub/Shutterstock, **33** (br) ZUMA Press, Inc./Alamy, **34** (br) Robynrg/Shutterstock, **35** PhotoAlto/Alamy, **36** (r) Artsilense/Shutterstock, **36** (cl), **36** (cr) Eric Isselee/Shutterstock, **36** (br) Erik Lam/Shutterstock, **36** (l) Alexia Khruscheva/Shutterstock, **37, 38–39** (t), **39** (cr), **40** Kenneth Garrett/NGC, **41** damnfx/NGC, **42–44** (t) age fotostock/Alamy, **42** (br), **43** (cr) Kenneth Garrett/NGC, **44** (cr) Seoul National University, **45** photopqr/La Depeche Du Midi/Newscom, **46–47, 48–50** (t) Gregory A. Harlin/NGC, **48** (br) Andrew Syred/Getty Images, **49** (br) Alexander Malee/NGC, **51** Stephen Alvarez/NGC, **52** (all) Stephen Alvarez/NGC, **53** Poras Chaudhary/Getty Images, **54** (t) Carol Beckwith & Angela Fisher/Robert Estall Photo Agency/Alamy, **54–55** (bkgd), **56–58** (t) hadynyah/Vetta/Getty Images, **56** (tr) Tischenko Irina/Shutterstock, **57** (cr) Roy Philippe/hemis.fr/Hemis/Alamy, **58** (cr) Frans Lemmens/Getty Images, **59** AFP/Getty Images, **60** (tr) China Photos/Getty Images, **60–61** (b), **62–64** (t), **62** (br) STR/AFP/Getty Images, **64** (cr) E J Davies/Getty Images, **65** (c) BioLife Pics/Shutterstock, **66, 113, 130, 143, 144, 190** National Geographic, **67** Craig Ruttle/Alamy, **70** (cl), **70–71** (b), **72–74** (t), **72** (cr) Stephen Alvarez/NGC, **74** (tr) Jacques Brinon/AP Images, **75** Tino Soriano/NGC, **76–77** Craig Ruttle/Alamy, **78–80** (t) Jannis Tobias Werner/Shutterstock, **78** (br) fivespots/Shutterstock, **79** (cr) Robert A. Sabo/Getty Images News/Getty Images, **80** (br) Pakhnyushcha/Shutterstock, **81** Daniel Aguilar/Reuters, **82** Carlos Jasso/AP Images, **83** Brian J. Skerry/NGC, **84–85** Tim Laman/NGC, **87** (bc) Rick Sass/NGC, **87** (br) James R.D. Scott/Getty Images, **87** (cr) Dickson Images/Getty Images, **88** (br) Prill/Shutterstock, **90** (cr) Brian J. Skerry/NGC, **91** Paul Sutherland/NGC, **92–93** (cr), **94–96** (t) Mauricio Handler/NGC, **94** (br) Bert Folsom/Alamy, **95** (br) Chris Ross/Aurora/Getty Images, **96** (br) Everett Collection, **97** Wayne Lynch/Getty Images, **98** Visual&Written SL/Alamy, **99** Joe Petersburger/NGC, **100–101** (t) Ton Koene/Horizons WWP/Alamy, **102** (t) Ton Koene/Alamy, **103** (tr), **103** (cr) Guillermo Legaria/AFP/Getty Images, **103** (br) Keith Levit/Alamy, **103** (bkgd) Lorraine Boogich/E+/Getty Images, **104–106** (t) catolla/Shutterstock, **104** (br) Lilyana Vynogradova/Shutterstock, **105** (cr) Pan Demin/Shutterstock, **107** (tl) Bright/Shutterstock, **107** (tc) Alex Norkin/Shutterstock, **107** (tr) Evgeny Dubinchuk/Shutterstock, **107** (cl) Kelly Vdv/Shutterstock, **107** (br) imagehub/Shutterstock, **108** Moirenc Camille/hemis.fr/Getty Images, **109** (tr) Paul Hawthorne/Getty Images Publicity/Getty Images, **109** (b) Picavet/Photolibrary/Getty Images, **110–112** (t) Roy Botterell/The Image Bank/Getty Images, **110** (cr) Danita Delimont/Gallo Images/Getty Images, **111** (cr) Florelena/Shutterstock, **112** (br) Michael Freeman/Aurora Photos, **114** (cl) rsooll/Shutterstock, **114** (cr) Martien van Gaalen/Shutterstock, **114** (bl) DmZ/Shutterstock, **114** (br) Alex Emanuel Koch/Shutterstock, **115** VisionsofAmerica/Joe Sohm/Digital Vision/Getty Images, **116–117** Rod Porteous/Alamy, **118–119, 120–122** (t) ZUMA Press/Newscom, **120** (cr) Andris Tkacenko/Shutterstock, **121** (br) Silvio Fiore/SuperStock, **122** (br) DeAgostini/SuperStock, **124** (t) Ignacio Palacios/Lonely Planet Images/Getty Images, **125** (t) Burt Silverman/NGC, **126–128** (t) Amar Grover/AWL Images/Getty Images, **126** (br) travelstock44/Look/Getty Images, **128** (br) Abraham Cresques/The Bridgeman Art Library/Getty Images, **129** (cr) Image Asset Management Ltd./SuperStock, **131** Erika Larsen/Redux, **132–133** Andrew Watson/Lonely Planet Images/Getty Images, **134** Catherine Karnow/NGC, **135–137** (t) Franz Pfluegl/Shutterstock, **135** (cr) Jorge Fajl/NGC, **136** (cr) Greg Dale/NGC, **137** (cr) AlinaStreltsova/Shutterstock, **138–139** (bkgd) Spectral-Design/Shutterstock, **138** (t) Mike Simons/Getty Images, **139** (cr) Michael Nichols/NGC, **140–142** (t) Jason Reed/Reuters, **140** (cr) Andrey Kuzmin/Shutterstock, **141** (tr) Christine Caldwell/Photolibrary/Getty Images, **142** (cr) Frazer Harrison/Staff/Getty Images Entertainment/Getty Images, **145** Michael Nolan/Robert Harding World Imagery/Getty Images, **148–149, 150–152** (t) Joe Raedle/Getty Images News/Getty Images, **150** (cr) Dmitry Deshevykh/E+/Getty Images, **151** (cr) Ralph Lee Hopkins/NGC, **154–155** David Mclain/NGC, **156–158** (t) Paul Nicklen/NGC, **156** (cr) Paul Souders/WorldFoto/The Image Bank/Getty Images, **157** (br) Sue Flood/The Image Bank/Getty Images, **158** (cr) Paul Souders/Stone/Getty Images, **161** Adegsm/Flickr Open/Getty Images, **162, 164–166** (t) Premaphotos/Alamy, **163** Malcolm Schuyl/Alamy, **164** (br) IrinaK/Shutterstock, **166** (bl) arlindo71/Getty Images, **167** (tl) Leo Shoot/Shutterstock, **167** (tr) Mircea Bezergheanu/Shutterstock, **167** (cl) Bruce MacQueen/Shutterstock, **168–169** (b), **170–172** (t) Ira Block/NGC, **169** (tr) Bonnie Taylor Barry/Shutterstock, **170** (cr) Joel Sartore/NGC, **171** (cr) Andreas Weitzmann/Shutterstock, **172** (br) Harold Wilion/Photolibrary/Getty Images, **173** (all) Daniel Dempster Photography/Alamy, **174** Tony Karumba/AFP/Getty Images, **175** Stephen Alvarez/NGC, **176** (tl) Margo Harrison/Shutterstock, **176** (cl) Barcroft Media/Getty Images, **177** Steven Robertson/E+/Getty Images, **178** (tr) Leonardo da Vinci/The Bridgeman Art Library/Getty Images, **178–179** AP Images/Bruno Brokken, **180–182** (t) Kazuhisa Akeo/a.collectionRF/Alamy, **180** (cr) Thomas Senf/Redbullnewsrooom/SIPA/Newscom, **181** (cr) Potapov Alexander/Shutterstock, **182** (cr) Red Bull Stratos/EPA/Newscom, **183** Frans Lanting/NGC, **184** Stephen Alvarez/NGC, **186–188** (t) Sisse Brimberg/NGC, **186** (br) Paul Nicklen/NGC, **187** (cr), **188** (cr) Stephen Alvarez/NGC, **189** Barcroft Media/Getty Images

NGC = National Geographic Creative

Illustration Credits

19 (all), **68–69, 70** (tr), **92** (b), **101** (cr), **102** (cr), **116** (c), **123** (t), **146–147, 153, 159, 185** National Geographic Maps

Text Credits

9 Adapted from "Sugar Love," by Rich Cohen: NGM, Aug 2013, **14** Adapted from "Food Ark," by Charles Siebert: NGM, Jul 2011, **23** Adapted from "What Are They Doing Down There?," and "Listening to Humpbacks," by Douglas Chadwick: NGM, Jan 2007/Jul 1999, **30** Adapted from "Wolf to Woof," by Karen Lange: NGM, Jan 2002, **39** Adapted from "Was King Tut Murdered?," by A. R. Williams: NGM, Jun 2005, **46** Adapted from "Last Hours of the Ice Man," by Stephen S. Hall: NGM, Jul 2007, **55** Adapted from "Brides of the Sahara," by Carol Beckwith and Angela Fisher: NGM, Feb 1998, **60** Adapted from "Battle for the Soul of Kung Fu," by Peter Gwin: NGM, Mar 2011, **69** Adapted from "Under Paris," by Neil Shea: NGM, Feb 2011, **75** Adapted from "Under New York," by Joel Swerdlow: NGM, Feb 1997, **85** Adapted from "Coral Reef Color," by Les Kaufman: NGM, May 2005, and "Coral in Peril," by Douglas Chadwick: NGM, Jan 1999, **92** Adapted from "Great White Deep Trouble," by Peter Benchley: NGM, Apr 2000, **101** Adapted from "Flower Trade," by Vivienne Walt: NGM, Apr 2001, **108** Adapted from "Perfume: The Essence of Illusion," by Cathy Newman: NGM, Oct 1998, **117** Adapted from "The Adventures of Marco Polo," by Mike Edwards: NGM, May–Jul 2001, **124** Adapted from "Ibn Battuta: Prince of Travelers," by Thomas J. Abercrombie: NGM, Dec 1991, **133** Adapted from "Beautiful Brains," by David Dobbs: NGM, Oct 2011, **139** Adapted from "A Thing or Two About Twins," by Peter Miller: NGM, Jan 2012, **147** Adapted from "The Big Thaw," by Tim Appenzeller: NGM, Jun 2007, **154** Adapted from "Last Days of the Ice Hunters," by Gretel Ehrlich: NGM, Jan 2006, **163** Adapted from "Army Ants," by Edward O. Wilson: NGM, Aug 2006, **168** Adapted from "Uncommon Vision," by Lynne Warren: NGM, May 2002, **177** Adapted from "If We Only Had Wings," by Nancy Shute: NGM, Sep 2011, **184** Adapted from "Call of the Abyss," by Alexander Klimchouk: NGM, May 2005

NGM = National Geographic Magazine

Acknowledgments

The Authors and Publisher would like to thank the following teaching professionals for their valuable feedback during the development of this series:

Ahmed Mohamed Motala, University of Sharjah; **Ana Laura Gandini**, Richard Anderson School; **Andrew T. Om**, YBM PINE R&D; **Dr. Asmaa Awad**, University of Sharjah; **Atsuko Takase**, Kinki University, Osaka; **Bogdan Pavliy**, Toyama University of International Studies; **Brigitte Maronde**, Harold Washington College, Chicago; **Bunleap Heap**, American Intercon Institute; **Carey Bray**, Columbus State University; **Carmella Lieske**, Shimane University; **Chanmakara Hok**, American Intercon Institute; **Choppie Tsann Tsang Yang**, National Taipei University; **Cynthia Ross**, State College of Florida; **David Schneer**, ACS International, Singapore; **Dawn Shimura**, St. Norbert College; **David Barrett**, Goldenwest College, CA; **Dax Thomas**, Keio University; **Deborah E. Wilson**, American University of Sharjah; **Elizabeth Rodacker**, Bakersfield College; **Emma Tamaianu-Morita**, Akita University; **Fu-Dong Chiou**, National Taiwan University; **Gavin Young**, Iwate University; **George Galamba**, Woodland Community College; **Gigi Santos**, American Intercon Institute; **Gursharan Kandola**, Language and Culture Center, University of Houston, TX; **Heidi Bundschoks**, ITESM, Sinaloa Mexico; **Helen E. Roland**, ESL/FL Miami-Dade College-Kendall Campus; **Hiroyo Yoshida**, Toyo University; **Hisayo Murase**, Doshisha Women's College of Liberal Arts; **Ikuko Kashiwabara**, Osaka Electro-Communication University; **J. Lorne Spry**, Contracting University Lecturer; **Jamie Ahn**, English Coach, Seoul; **Jane Bergmann**, The University of Texas at San Antonio; **Jennie Farnell**, University of Connecticut; **José Olavo de Amorim**, Colegio Bandeirantes, Sao Paulo; **Kyoungnam Shon**, Avalon English; **Luningning C. Landingin**, American Intercon Institute; **Mae-Ran Park**, Pukyong National University, Busan; **Mai Minh Tiên**, Vietnam Australia International School; **Marina Gonzalez**, Instituto Universitario de Lenguas Modernas Pte., Buenos Aires; **Mark Rau**, American River College, Sacramento CA; **Max Heineck**, Academic Coordinator/Lecturer, King Fahd University of Petroleum & Minerals; **Dr. Melanie Gobert**, Higher Colleges of Technology; **Michael C. Cheng**, National Chengchi University; **Michael Johnson**, Muroran Institute of Technology; **Michael McGuire**, Kansai Gaidai University; **Muriel Fujii**, University of Hawaii; **Patrick Kiernan**, Meiji University; **Philip Suthons**, Aichi Shukutoku University; **Renata Bobakova**, English Programs for Internationals, Columbia, SC; **Rhonda Tolhurst**, Kanazawa University; **Rodney Johnson**, Kansai Gaidai University; **Rosa Enilda Vásquez Fernandez**, John F. Kennedy Institute of Languages, Inc.; **Sandra Kern**, New Teacher Coach, School District of Philadelphia; **Shaofang Wu**, National Cheng Kung University; **Sovathey Tim**, American Intercon Institute; **Stephen Shrader**, Notre Dame Seishin Women's University; **Sudeepa Gulati**, Long Beach City College; **Susan Orias**, Broward College; **Thays Ladosky**, Colegio Damas, Recife; **Thea Chan**, American Intercon Institute; **Tom Justice**, North Shore Community College; **Tony J.C. Carnerie**, UCSD English Language Institute; **Tsung-Yuan Hsiao**, National Taiwan Ocean University, Keelung; **Virginia Christopher**, University of Calgary-Qatar; **Vuthy Lorn**, American Intercon Institute; **Wm Troy Tucker**, Edison State College; **Yohei Murayama**, Kagoshima University; **Yoko Sakurai**, Aichi University; **Yoko Sato**, Tokyo University of Agriculture and Technology